INTRODUCING
SCHOLARLY RESEARCH

ALA Editions purchases fund advocacy, awareness,
and accreditation programs for library professionals worldwide.

INTRODUCING SCHOLARLY RESEARCH

READY-TO-USE LESSON PLANS AND ACTIVITIES FOR UNDERGRADUATES

Toni Carter

CHICAGO | 2022

TONI CARTER is director of Kares Library at Athens State University in Athens, Alabama. Until recently, her fifteen-year career in academic librarianship has focused on information literacy instruction, having served as both an instruction librarian and instruction coordinator. She has published peer-reviewed articles and has presented related topics at local, regional, and national conferences, including the ACRL, ALA, and LOEX.

© 2022 by Toni Carter

Extensive effort has gone into ensuring the reliability of the information in this book; however, the publisher makes no warranty, express or implied, with respect to the material contained herein.

ISBN: 978-0-8389-3782-2 (paper)

Library of Congress Cataloging-in-Publication Data
Names: Carter, Toni M., author.
Title: Introducing scholarly research : ready-to-use lesson plans and activities for undergraduates / Toni Carter.
Description: Chicago : ALA Editions, 2022. | Includes bibliographical references and index. | Summary: "With over 30 time-saving lesson plans, this book will provide you with tools and activities for your information literacy instruction"—Provided by publisher.
Identifiers: LCCN 2021016608 | ISBN 9780838937822 (paperback)
Subjects: LCSH: Information literacy—Study and teaching (Higher)—Activity programs. | Academic libraries—Relations with faculty and curriculum.
Classification: LCC ZA3088.5.C65 C37 2022 | DDC 028.7071/173—dc23
LC record available at https://lccn.loc.gov/2021016608

Cover design by Kimberly Hudgins. Cover images © Adobe Stock.
Text design and composition by Karen Sheets de Gracia in the Mercury, Bebas, and Gotham typefaces.

♾ This paper meets the requirements of ANSI/NISO Z39.48-1992 (Permanence of Paper).

PRINTED IN THE UNITED STATES OF AMERICA

26 25 24 23 22   5 4 3 2 1

*For my mom and dad, who have always offered
unwavering encouragement.*

CONTENTS

List of Worksheets *ix*
Preface *xi*
Acknowledgments *xiii*
Introduction *xv*

1 / PROCESS *1*

Lesson 1: Research Happens . . . But Why? *2*
Lesson 2: A Malleable (and Messy) Process *6*
Lesson 3: The Conversations of Scholars *9*
Lesson 4: Peer Review as the Gold Standard *12*
Lesson 5: Markers of Authority *16*
Lesson 6: Sharing the Results *20*

2 / PEOPLE *25*

Lesson 7: What Is a Scholar? *26*
Lesson 8: Paths to a PhD *29*
Lesson 9: Diversity among Scholars *33*
Lesson 10: Community-Granted Authority *36*
Lesson 11: Uses for Scholarly Profiles *40*
Lesson 12: Inclusivity and the Scholarly Conversation *43*
Conversation Starters *47*

3 / TERMINOLOGY *51*

Lesson 13: A Lexicon Exists *52*
Lesson 14: Stay Calm and Choose the Right Words *55*
Lesson 15: *Scholarly*: Exploring a Fundamental Term *59*
Lesson 16: Is It a *Search* or Is It *Research*? *62*

4 / METHODS OF INQUIRY *67*

Lesson 17: Scientific Method: One Size Fits All? *68*
Lesson 18: Research Design *72*
Lesson 19: The Two Qs of Research *77*
Conversation Starters *81*

5 / DISCIPLINES *89*

Lesson 20: Start with the Liberal Arts *90*
Lesson 21: Science Research: The Familiar *96*
Lesson 22: Social Science Research: The Less Familiar *100*
Lesson 23: Digital Humanities *104*
Conversation Starters *108*

6 / DISSEMINATION AND ACCESS *109*

Lesson 24: The Job of Scholarly Journals *110*
Lesson 25: Choosing Where to Publish *113*
Lesson 26: Subscriptions to Scholarly Research *117*
Lesson 27: Open Access *121*
Conversation Starters *126*

7 / ON CAMPUS *133*

Lesson 28: The Research University *134*
Lesson 29: Show Me the Grant Money *137*
Lesson 30: Protecting Humans *141*
Lesson 31: The Value of the Library *145*
Lesson 32: Undergraduate Research *149*
Lesson 33: Publish or Perish *154*

Bibliography *159*
Index *161*

WORKSHEETS

1.1	Purposes of Scholarly Research	5
1.2	Peer-Review Process Roles	15
1.3	My Professor's Authority	19
2.1	Education of Professionals	32
2.2	Gaining Authority	39
2.3	Scholarly Profile	42
2.4	Barriers to Inclusivity	46
3.1	Research Scenarios	64
4.1	Does One Size Fit All?	71
4.2	Designing a House	75
4.3	Designing Research	76
4.4	QUAN or QUAL	80
5.1	Humanists	93
5.2	Social Scientists	94
5.3	Natural Scientists	95
5.4	Comparing Research in the Sciences	99
5.5	Value of the Social Sciences	102
5.6	Digital Humanities Project	107
6.1	Conversations and Communication	112
6.2	Choosing a Scholarly Journal	116
6.3	Journal Subscriptions	120
6.4	Open Access Policies	124
7.1	Research Grants	140
7.2	Human Subjects	144
7.3	List of Library Services	148
7.4	Undergraduate Research	152
7.5	Tenure Requirements	157

PREFACE

I cannot call myself a first-generation college student. My mother attended a two-year trade school, and my father returned to college during my teenage years to complete a bachelor's degree he had begun prior to my birth. In fact, he and I graduated the same semester from the same state teaching college. Obviously, I benefited from privilege as I entered college at eighteen, but I entered with an almost nonexistent understanding of the research aspects of higher education. My assumptions about college involved sitting in class, absorbing lectures, taking notes, regurgitating notes, graduating in four years, and then finding a job. Looking back, my perception was not that far off. While I enjoyed my courses and admired my professors, I recollect no discussions in class about how to conduct scholarly research, and I certainly have no memories of instruction sessions with friendly and knowledgeable librarians. If I absorbed any part of the scholarly research ecosystem during my undergraduate years, it was the value of a PhD. In a very roundabout way, that one piece of knowledge resulted in my becoming an academic librarian. I was woefully unprepared for graduate school, though. My writing skills were lacking and my research consisted of fumbling around on JSTOR. I stuck with it, though, learned more about the research ecosystem, and graduated with two master's degrees.

I tell this story because whenever I run across an undergraduate student who is already plugged into the research community on campus, I think "How did this student get a leg up?" Twenty years after my college experiences, I see myself in a subset of the undergraduates. Some arrive on campus ahead of the game, and others will need to catch up. I identify with the latter. My time as an undergraduate (and graduate student) clearly influence how I interact with students today—in a positive way, I hope. Even those students who seem "plugged in," however, know only a fraction of the research story.

I have taught hundreds of one-shot library instruction sessions during my time as an academic librarian. For the most part, these sessions have centered on teaching first-year students a handful of basic information literacy skills; for example, how to conduct a keyword search in library databases, how to locate peer-reviewed articles, and in the early days of the internet, sessions on website evaluation. Over the years, I grew to recognize that despite our best efforts at first-year instruction and discipline-specific research instruction later in their college careers, students still lacked a complete understanding of the big picture in regard to scholarly research.

An opportunity for me to explore this concern, as well as to expand my teaching repertoire, emerged in the form of a newly approved, three-credit-hour honors course on research methods. The course lacked an instructor, and I jumped at the chance. The approved syllabus for the course defined *research methods* broadly to include topics such as quantitative and qualitative research methods, ethics, disciplinary research practices, the campus infrastructure that supports research, and grant-writing. With the freedom to put my own spin on the course, I set out to stay true to the spirit of the syllabus, but not overwhelm what turned out to be a large number of first- and second-year students. As I planned for the course and searched for textbooks and course readings, I realized that what I sought not only did not conveniently exist in one textbook, but some of the topics lacked any instructional guidance whatsoever. I began referring to this hodgepodge of themes that I needed to stitch together as the *scholarly research ecosystem*. Though I had never heard this phrase before, no doubt others have used it before me. Out of frustration but also curiosity, I decided to write a book that could be used to teach students about the scholarly research ecosystem.

I planned to begin and finish this book while simultaneously teaching my first semester of the research methods course. This fantastical plan stretched through a second semester and part of a third, but the delay resulted in a better product, I believe. I considered the course a nonscientific experiment, and it was one that confirmed my suspicions. Undergraduates (at least the small sample that I had access to) lacked knowledge of critical parts of the scholarly research ecosystem. And given the fact that these were honors students who proactively sought out research opportunities on campus, their gaps in knowledge suggested an even greater deficit among typical undergraduates.

In this volume I present commentary and teaching ideas based on what I learned in that immersive instructional experience, framed by my fifteen years of information literacy and library instruction experience. I point out particular assumptions that students make regarding the scholarly research ecosystem. I also identify what they understand well, and those areas in which they are deficient. Some of the activities offered in this book will be more appropriate for students who plan to attend graduate school. Most of the lessons, however, treat concepts and processes within the scholarly research ecosystem that all undergraduates should know—especially if they are required to conduct scholarly research.

ACKNOWLEDGMENTS

I can only put my thoughts to paper in this volume because so many people in the academic library profession have inspired me over the last twenty years through conversations, collaborations, and scholarship. I am fortunate to be part of such a generous group of professionals. I owe a tremendous debt of gratitude to a few individuals in particular for supporting my work as a librarian, and I humbly thank them here.

Frances Pollard, retired librarian at the Virginia Historical Society, took a chance on me as a brand-new MLIS graduate in 2001. Her definition of professionalism I carry with me to this day.

Priscilla Seaman, a fellow reference and instruction librarian during my time at the University of Tennessee at Chattanooga, became a lifelong friend, sharing the highs and lows of life in and out of the library. Priscilla is currently a senior assistant librarian at the University Libraries, University at Albany, SUNY.

At Auburn University Libraries, Nancy Noe, my predecessor as instruction coordinator, has been a steadfast mentor, and more than anyone has helped to shape my perspectives on librarianship and information literacy. Emulating her dedication to simplicity and common-sense thinking has been a consistent ambition of mine as I navigate the roles of academic, faculty member, librarian, and teacher.

Marcia Boosinger, retired associate dean of public services and head of reference and instruction, and Claudine Jenda, the current interim head of research and instruction services, supported my promotion and tenure journey, believed in my ideas along the way, and gave me space to practice my leadership skills. I have shared an office wall with Dr. Juliet Rumble, the religion and philosophy librarian, for ten years. During this time, I have admired and hopefully absorbed a fraction of her keen editing skills. To my other colleagues in the Research and Instruction Services Department, I have valued your support and friendship throughout the years, your encouragement and constructive criticism when the situation called for either, and your commitment to graduating information-literate students. These colleagues include Jaena Alabi, Barbara Bishop, Dr. Rob Buchanan (retired), Dr. Tim Dodge, Adelia Grabowsky, Patricia Hartman, Ali Krzton, Kasia Leousis, Todd Shipman, Liza Weisbrod, and Andrew Wohrley. I extend this sentiment to Bridget Farrell and Pam Whaley as well, who have moved on to other institutions. I am appreciative of all of the staff and faculty at Auburn University Libraries for helping me to do my job.

Lastly, in fall 2019, a small group of students enrolled in the first for-credit research methods course for which I was the instructor of record. Madeline Matheson, Chloe Moore, Emma Kate Seckinger, and Brandon Thomas, thank you for demonstrating patience as we learned together. No doubt you will do great things in this world. My appreciation goes out to Dr. Tiffany Sippial as well, who directs the university's Honors College, for giving me the chance to teach that course.

I am a better librarian because of all of the individuals listed above. This book, however, is a work of my own, and I take sole responsibility for its errors and shortcomings.

INTRODUCTION

The scholarly research ecosystem encompasses all facets of scholarly research, and this book aims to provide lesson ideas for many of these facets. The book includes concepts grounded in the *Framework for Information Literacy for Higher Education* that involve the research process, as well as research design and methods, the language and specialized vocabulary of scholarly research, the roles and expectations of scholars who conduct the research, and the units and services that support scholarly research.[1] Librarians address some of these topics during library and information literacy instruction sessions, particularly those found in the *Framework*. Students might gain exposure to some of the other concepts, such as research design and methods, in their discipline-specific courses. I would argue, however, that college students rarely receive intentional and systematic instruction on most aspects of the scholarly research ecosystem. Of course, some may question whether undergraduates need this kind of in-depth instruction unless they plan to attend graduate school. My counterargument would center on the well-worn statement that "knowledge is power." Is it fair to require students to search for scholarly materials when they lack an understanding of the systems in place that disseminate the research? What about the sociopolitical issues that can limit diverse voices within scholarly conversations? Let's try to imagine how offering undergraduates more context about the "big picture" (i.e., the scholarly research ecosystem) might influence how they locate, evaluate, use, think about, and conduct their own scholarly research.

As librarians, what stands in our way from enlightening undergraduates with this kind of information? Limited opportunities in the classroom, limited access to students, and limited control over the curriculum most likely play a part. For those constrained by one-shots, the design of this book should allow you to pick and choose lessons as needed. Most lessons will fit within a fifty-minute one-shot session. And under strict time constraints, many of the activities *within* the lessons could stand on their own. This modular design allows for mixing and matching. For those of you with a penchant for pushing the envelope, this book can also serve as a tool for lobbying for more research instruction for students. We know that instructors and faculty tend to overestimate what undergraduates know about research. You can share this book with discipline-specific faculty and administrators. Ask them to identify topics they recognize as areas of weakness or spheres of misinformation for undergraduates. Push for train-the-trainer events for faculty and suggest aspects of the scholarly research ecosystem that particular groups of students would benefit from knowing. Maybe this is wishful thinking, but I believe the lessons in this book could serve as a curriculum model for courses devoted to teaching the scholarly research ecosystem.

STYLE OF TEACHING

Our profession has produced many creative and clever strategies for teaching generic information literacy skills such as how to find scholarly articles in a library database or identifying peer-reviewed articles.[2] The lessons in this book take a slightly different approach, with less focus on teaching discrete skills and more emphasis on having students answer the *why*, as in *"why* do scholars use library databases?" or *"why* is peer review important to scholarly research?" The instructional strategies presented here are no doubt influenced by my personal pedagogical style—the one I have developed through my teaching experiences in both one-shot and for-credit courses, through my professional training, such as participation in the Association of College & Research Libraries' Immersion Program, and by observing other librarians teach. The lessons in this book encourage active learning and student engagement. Many of the lessons involve class discussion and therefore call for the flexibility to go "off-script" at times. If you are uncomfortable with this approach, you can revise the lessons to fit your own teaching style and students' needs. Also, in the wake of the global pandemic that resulted in so many of us transitioning from in-person to virtual instruction, these lessons lend themselves to compatibility with online educational technologies that encourage active and participatory learning.

THINKING AT THE LOCAL LEVEL

Not all undergraduates come to the table with the same set of skills, nor do they enter college with the same set of objectives. Acknowledging these differences can make for a more inclusive learning environment. At the institutional level, we often fail to respond fully or accurately to the needs of our less privileged students, but you can do your part to correct this. You should take into account the historical backgrounds and current socio-economic circumstances of your students when using the lessons. Change the examples to resonate with the undergraduates sitting in front of you. Experiment with ways to gently encourage the involvement of all students in class discussions, not just those who speak up without being called on. If it helps with engagement, you can transform group activities into classroom competitions. Matters such as these require from you a sensitivity to individual student needs and classroom dynamics, skills difficult to nurture through one-shot sessions. The solution to this is both practice and frank communication with instructors about these issues prior to sessions.

Along with the uniqueness of your students, the content in some of the lessons may not align perfectly with the scholarly research ecosystem at your institution. For instance, if you teach at a college or university that prioritizes teaching or other faculty activities over scholarly research output, undergraduates may have fewer opportunities to witness aspects of the ecosystem in action. In addition, this book tends to emphasize research in the liberal arts, which may seem irrelevant to those of you who teach undergraduates in professional programs, such as nursing and education. Whichever of these issues you might identify with, with a bit of creativity—which overflows from librarians—the activities in this book can be adapted to fit your situation. Note: because the term *scholar* has such heavy use in the book, I feel it necessary to point out that this word can be replaced with *researcher, professor, faculty member*—whatever best aligns with your local situation.

Lastly, access to specific types of classroom technology and supplies referred to in this book may not be available to you. If you lack an endless supply of paper for worksheets, create online forms instead. For the reverse circumstance, you can gather student responses with the use of abandoned card catalog cards rather than with online audience-response tools. Have a shortage of whiteboards? Use easel pads. Whatever the perceived obstacle, making adjustments to ensure an inclusive and accessible learning environment for all students in the context of these lessons should be achievable.

WORDS MATTER

Consider a scenario in which you underestimate the amount of beige-colored paint needed for a home improvement project. You send your partner to the store to purchase more. Rather than beige-colored paint, however, they return with taupe-colored paint because, according to them, it was on sale and the color seemed "close enough." Now, imagine that your supervisor asks you to prepare a presentation on the projected growth of online education over the next five years. After creating the presentation, you discover that your supervisor equates online education with distance education; in other words, students take courses at a "distance" from campus. You, on the other hand, define *online education* as any student who takes a course online, regardless of where they live. The first scenario serves as a metaphor; the colors may have a similar hue, but they are not the same, just as words that are closely related are not necessarily synonyms. The second scenario illustrates an outcome of misinterpreting or assuming word meaning. Clearly, neither scenario would be described as a life-or-death situation, and the subtle variations in meaning may seem inconsequential.

How does this relate to scholarly research? Because librarians have such limited opportunities to interface with students, we tend to conflate different terms. For instance, a jury would find me guilty of using the words *scholarly*, *academic*, and *peer-reviewed* synonymously. This book contains four lessons dedicated to the language of scholarly research. You might consider that a bit excessive, but due to my experiences working with students, I now tend to obsess over the words I choose to use in the classroom. Words *do* matter. No doubt I have conflated some similar words and concepts in this book. However, where it matters, I have been particularly careful with my choice of words. If you are fortunate enough to have the opportunity, asking undergraduates to immerse themselves in the terminology of scholarly research can only strengthen their critical thinking skills and their understanding of the scholarly research ecosystem.

LESSON OUTLINE

Each lesson follows a similar outline.

SUMMARY: The summary will give you a brief overview of the purpose of the lesson, as well as the type of activities it includes.

SKILL LEVEL: In the absence of a rubric or other more exacting measures, determining the skill level of students and whether that aligns with a particular lesson can prove subjective and heavily dependent on local circumstances. As a benchmark, I consider the lessons labeled as *novice* as suitable for most first-year college students.

CONTEXT: Each lesson includes a paragraph to help situate the topic within the scholarly research ecosystem and how undergraduates would benefit from the lesson.

LEARNING OUTCOME: Each lesson centers on an adaptable learning outcome.

PREPARATION: Lists of needed supplies and descriptions of necessary preplanning have been included in the "Preparation" section of each lesson. In some cases, I offer additional or alternative ideas for the activities.

INSTRUCTION: Each lesson includes two activities that consist of class discussion, individual work, and group work. In *most* cases, the first activity introduces the topic using a real-world example relevant to students, and the second activity places the topic within the context of scholarly research. Estimates on the duration of each activity are included.

ASSESSMENT PROMPT: The assessment prompts function as informal and quick methods to measure student understanding, with the purpose of providing feedback that helps you improve the lesson. Appropriate and relevant examples of these types of assessments can be found in the book *Classroom Assessment Techniques for Librarians*.[3]

CONVERSATION STARTERS

Although this book provides thirty-three lessons related to the scholarly research ecosystem, there are many more topics concerning scholarly research that could be relevant to undergraduates. Therefore, some chapters of this book offer questions about additional concepts in order to spark ideas for classroom discussions and activities, as well as full lessons.

NOTES

1. Association of College & Research Libraries, *Framework for Information Literacy for Higher Education*, 2015, www.ala.org/acrl/standards/ilframework.
2. Mandy Lupton and Christine Susan Bruce, "Windows on Information Literacy Worlds: Generic, Situated and Transformative Perspectives," in *Practising Information Literacy: Bringing Theories of Learning, Practice and Information Literacy Together*, ed. Annemaree Lloyd and Sanna Talja (Wagga Wagga, New South Wales: Charles Stuart University, 2010), 3–27.
3. Melissa Bowles-Terry and Cassandra Kvenild, *Classroom Assessment Techniques for Librarians* (Chicago: Association of College & Research Libraries, 2015).

CHAPTER 1

PROCESS

The lessons in this chapter cover key components of the research process and are aligned with concepts described in particular frames of the *Framework for Information Literacy for Higher Education*, such as "Authority Is Constructed and Contextual," "Information Creation as a Process," "Research as Inquiry," and "Scholarship as Conversation."[1] While the lessons in this chapter may be familiar instruction topics on information literacy used by librarians, they aim to provide new or alternative activities to meet the student learning outcomes.

LESSON 1

RESEARCH HAPPENS ... BUT WHY?

SUMMARY

In this lesson, students engage in discussion about the purposes of scholarly research. They analyze abstracts from peer-reviewed articles as one strategy for identifying the purposes of scholarly research.

SKILL LEVEL

Novice to Intermediate

CONTEXT

When asked to describe the purpose of scholarly research, the responses from undergraduates will likely fall into two categories. The first category consists of specific areas of research, particularly ones that society has deemed as important. Responses might include curing cancer or reversing global warming. The second category, and the motivation for this lesson, involves responses that define the broad purposes of research, particularly solving problems and discovering something new; or, as they are known in the scholarly research ecosystem, applied research and basic research, respectively. We know, however, that when presented with categories of "things," especially two "things," students have a tendency for absolute thinking. Despite our most earnest pleas, they could walk away believing that the purpose of *all* research is *either* problem-solving *or* discovery. Hence, you should encourage students to brainstorm various purposes of research in the first activity, with the understanding that this lesson focuses only on two of them. In addition, problem-solving and discovery tend to imply the natural sciences and the social sciences. Although this viewpoint is not discouraged, if you use research topics from the humanities, consider the inclusion of a third reason for scholarly research, such as "for the betterment of society or civilization."

LEARNING OUTCOME

The students will analyze abstracts from peer-reviewed articles in order to articulate the purposes of scholarly research.

PREPARATION

To prepare for the session, create a free-form survey using an audience-response tool with the prompt: "What are the purposes of scholarly research?" Choose two abstracts from peer-reviewed articles: one study that attempts to solve a problem, and one with the purpose of discovering something new. Choose abstracts that undergraduates can comprehend despite their probable lack of expertise on the topic; examples within the same research area would be best. Make enough copies of these abstracts for each pair of students. In addition, prepare a copy of the "Purposes of Scholarly Research" worksheet (worksheet 1.1) for each student. Additional ideas as you prepare:

- As an alternative to producing paper worksheets, create an online form that populates the students' responses into a spreadsheet. This way, students can enter their responses to the worksheet, and their answers can be shared with the class in real time.
- For an abbreviated version of the lesson, each pair of students could work with just one of the abstracts. For instance, groups one and two would receive "Abstract 1" and groups three and four would receive "Abstract 2."
- You may need to explain the purpose of an abstract, depending on the level of the class.
- To reduce the chance that students internalize the misconception that reading the abstract can substitute for reading the article, ask them to review the entire article, not just the abstract.
- For advanced undergraduates, introduce the formal descriptors of applied and basic research.

INSTRUCTION

ACTIVITY ONE: IDENTIFYING THE PURPOSES OF SCHOLARLY RESEARCH

Individual work, class discussion, 10 to 15 minutes

Using the audience-response tool, ask each student to enter their answer to the question "What is the purpose of scholarly research?" The answers should display in real time on the screen. The students will most likely come up with similar responses; ask the class to choose two or three common themes from their responses. Guide the students to identify *solving a problem* and *discovering something new* (or *discovery*) as two main purposes.

ACTIVITY TWO: PURPOSES THROUGH ABSTRACTS

Group work, class discussion, 15 to 20 minutes

Each pair of students will receive a copy of both abstracts, along with two "Purposes of Scholarly Research" worksheets (worksheet 1.1). Instruct each student in a pair to choose one abstract and complete the top half of the worksheet under the heading "Abstract 1." When complete, ask the students to swap abstracts with their partners and complete the activity once again, filling in the bottom half of the worksheet under the heading "Abstract 2." When finished, each pair of students will review their answers and come to an agreement on the purpose of the research for each example. Call on the pairs to justify their choices, and then try to bring the discussion back around to the themes identified at the beginning of the session. Emphasize the importance of both types of research.

ASSESSMENT

Students explain the purposes of research as covered in this lesson.

WORKSHEET 1.1

PURPOSES OF SCHOLARLY RESEARCH

Analyze your assigned abstracts and answer the following questions based on your analysis.

ABSTRACT 1

a. Do the author/s state the purpose of their research? If so, what is it?

b. Who will this research benefit? For instance, a group of people, an industry, the environment? Does that help to identify the purpose of the research? Explain.

c. Using the themes identified in our earlier activity and based on your analysis above, what do you believe is the purpose of this research?

ABSTRACT 2

a. Do the author/s state the purpose of their research? If so, what is it?

b. Who will this research benefit? For instance, a group of people, an industry, the environment? Does that help to identify the purpose of the research? Explain.

c. Using the themes identified in our earlier activity and based on your analysis above, what do you believe is the purpose of this research?

LESSON 2

A MALLEABLE (AND MESSY) PROCESS

SUMMARY

The students work in groups to visualize the organization of the research process. They come together to share how they imagined the process and adjust their original work based on the discussion.

SKILL LEVEL

Novice to Intermediate

CONTEXT

While current literature and the *Framework for Information Literacy for Higher Education* stress the iterative nature of the scholarly research process, this lesson stops short of introducing that particular terminology.[2] Instead, students explore various parts of the process and consider for themselves how these parts might be organized. After completion of this lesson, they should begin to recognize the messiness or flexibility of the scholarly research process. Note that the use of the word *parts* rather than *steps* in this lesson is intentional. Although this activity does not emphasize the linear versus iterative issue, you may not want to encourage linear thought, and words such as *steps* and *stages* tend to indicate a linear process.

LEARNING OUTCOME

Students will consider parts of the scholarly research process in order to recognize that the process can play out in different ways.

PREPARATION

Each group of three to four students will need a folder that contains descriptions of about seven or eight various parts of the scholarly research process, printed on separate pieces of paper. Examples of parts of the research process include: choose a topic, develop a research question, search for previous research, choose a journal in which to publish, revise the research question, ask a colleague to proofread your paper, sketch out an outline for your paper, choose a research design, write a grant to help fund your research, and publicize your research.

For these examples, you should determine whether you want this research process to align with how students research and write their papers, or go beyond that, and include additional parts that make up the research process of scholars. This latter option could include grant funding and publicizing scholarly work and may not include more basic elements such as "choose a topic." Inference should allow students to take part in this activity regardless of their level of familiarity with all of the examples. In addition to the examples, include at least five pieces of blank paper in each folder. Plan to provide the groups with adhesive appropriate for classroom walls or whiteboards.

Here are some additional ideas as you prepare:

- Assign each group a research scenario so that students can consider how the research process varies based on the situation or topic.
- Ask the students to compare their own research process to that of scholars or discipline-specific experts.
- Rather than using paper, volunteers act as the "parts" of the research process. Ask them to physically organize themselves at the front of the room based on directions given by their classmates.

INSTRUCTION

ACTIVITY ONE: ORGANIZING THE SCHOLARLY RESEARCH PROCESS

Group work, class discussion, 10 to 15 minutes

Form groups of three or four students each and provide each group with a pre-prepared folder and adhesive. Ask the students to review the contents of the folders, and to discuss among themselves how the different parts of the research process might be organized. Each group will then tape their paper on the wall in a design that reflects their discussion and vision. The pieces of paper will most likely be displayed in a straight line, to indicate linearity. Ask the students to use the blank pieces of paper to add at least three additional stages, or to duplicate parts of the process that could occur more than once. After students complete this exercise, have each group briefly share with the class how they organized the research process. This activity should emphasize to students that although all scholars may work through similar stages, the order of those stages can vary from one person and situation to the next.

ACTIVITY TWO: ANALYZING THE SCHOLARLY RESEARCH PROCESS

Class discussion, group work, 15 to 20 minutes

Lead a class discussion based on the work done in the previous activity, using this prompt: "For the activity that you just completed, there isn't an exact right or wrong answer. Why is that?"

Here are some more questions to help guide the discussion:

- Does the lack of a standard research process complicate research? Why or why not? Now consider the opposite position. How could this lack benefit scholars who conduct research?
- Which parts of the research process could or should be done multiple times?
- Based on how each group organized their process on the wall, which parts did most of you agree should happen at a certain time during the research process? Which parts vary the most between groups?
- Do you think this process differs from discipline to discipline? Explain.

Following the class discussion, give the students a second attempt to organize their processes on the wall. Allow them to add an additional two parts if they feel like they left something out during the first round. You should expect changes made based on the class discussion, but the groups should still visualize their processes in diverse ways, reinforcing the learning outcome.

ASSESSMENT PROMPT

"Sometimes you may hear people refer to the scholarly research process as *messy*. Do you think that's a fair description? Why or why not?"

LESSON 3

THE CONVERSATIONS OF SCHOLARS

SUMMARY

Students consider the types of conversations they take part in and compare those to scholarly conversations. They examine the "Scholarship as Conversation" frame from the *Framework* in order to learn more about how scholars communicate with each other.[3]

SKILL LEVEL

Intermediate to Advanced

CONTEXT

As early as first-year writing courses, well-meaning instructors develop assignments that require undergraduates to "join the scholarly conversation." The assignments go something like this: students choose a topic, select three peer-reviewed articles about that topic, synthesize those articles in the form of a research paper, and add their own voice—often described as a "new" perspective—to the conversation. What results is an exercise in futility; first-year students can rarely claim expertise in any topics in which peer-reviewed studies exist, and so they struggle to find their place in this type of "conversation." Yet, for some reason, we continue to disregard this deficit, expecting novice researchers to effectively join and contribute to scholarly conversations in fields they know little about. Meanwhile, instruction on the purpose and importance of the scholarly conversation to the research ecosystem gets overshadowed by students' frantic search for three peer-reviewed articles. Undergraduates need adequate exposure to the concept of the scholarly conversation before we ask them to join one. This lesson attempts to provide that exposure with the use of the "Scholarship as Conversation" frame from the ACRL's *Framework for Information Literacy for Higher Education*.

LEARNING OUTCOME

Students will study the "Scholarship as Conversation" frame in order to learn about the purpose of the scholarly conversation.

PREPARATION

Be equipped to display to the class a copy of the *Framework for Information Literacy for Higher Education*. Each student will need a copy of the "Scholarship as Conversation" handout (box 1.1), a highlighter or pencil, and a note card.

INSTRUCTION

ACTIVITY ONE: DEFINING THE SCHOLARLY CONVERSATION

Class discussion, 15 to 20 minutes

Begin a dialogue with students about how they contribute to online discussions through social media, blogs, comment sections, and so on. For instance, do they share opinions, correct misinformation, bring new facts to the conversation, and so on? Introduce the idea that by interacting with others in this way, they contribute to a larger conversation that may include many people. If possible, use a conversation that is relevant to the particular group of students as an example. Emphasize the pace of these types of conversations and the speed at which some of these conversations take place (this can later be compared with the slower speed of traditional scholarly conversations, such as through peer review).

Now, ask the students to add the term *scholarly* to *conversation*, as in a *scholarly conversation*. Solicit responses to the following questions:

- Does the addition of the word *scholarly* change the meaning of the conversation? If so, how?
- Have you heard of this phrase before in other courses? If so, what did it mean in that context?
- Do scholarly conversations happen the same way as other types of conversations? Explain.

ACTIVITY TWO: READING THE "SCHOLARSHIP AS CONVERSATION" FRAME

Individual work, class discussion, 20 to 25 minutes

On one side of their note card, ask each student to write down their understanding of the purpose of the scholarly conversation. Explain that they will return to the note card later.

At this point, display the *Framework* document and, for context, briefly explain the role that librarians play in helping students learn about the concept of "scholarship as conversation." You may want to take a moment and allow students to make the connection between the "scholarly conversation" and "scholarship as conversation." Provide each student with a copy of the pre-prepared excerpt from the "Scholarship as Conversation" frame (box 1.1). Instruct

SCHOLARSHIP AS CONVERSATION

"Research in scholarly and professional fields is a discursive practice in which ideas are formulated, debated, and weighed against one another over extended periods of time. Instead of seeking discrete answers to complex problems, experts understand that a given issue may be characterized by several competing perspectives as part of an ongoing conversation in which information users and creators come together and negotiate meaning. Experts understand that, while some topics have established answers through this process, a query may not have a single uncontested answer. Experts are therefore inclined to seek out many perspectives, not merely the ones with which they are familiar. These perspectives might be in their own discipline or profession or may be in other fields."

—From *Framework for Information Literacy for Higher Education*

BOX 1.1 "Scholarship as Conversation" handout

the students to highlight or circle the words or phrases in the excerpt that seem critical to understanding the concept of "scholarship as conversation."

Lead a discussion about their highlighted words and phrases. You have several options for what to focus on. For example, the terms *discursive, extended periods of time, discrete answers, competing perspectives,* and *negotiate* all play a part in the description of "scholarship as conversation." For a different approach, rather than students highlighting "words or phrases that they consider critical to understanding the concept of *scholarly conversation,*" ask them to highlight unfamiliar words or phrases. This strategy should still result in an equally productive discussion. In addition, for a more in-depth lesson or a possible assignment, identify a scholarly conversation for students to examine for evidence of the characteristics described in the "Scholarship as Conversation" frame.

ASSESSMENT PROMPT

"Return to your original description of the purpose of a scholarly conversation. Flip the note card over and indicate whether your description has changed due to our class discussion today. Explain why or why not."

LESSON 4

PEER REVIEW AS THE GOLD STANDARD

SUMMARY

Students critically examine the purpose of the peer-review process and take a deep dive into the peer-review publication process with the help of role-playing.

SKILL LEVEL

Novice to Intermediate

CONTEXT

Peer review is the evaluation of scientific and other intellectual work by qualified members of a profession who are working in the same field. The review is designed to assess the accuracy, validity, and originality of papers that are candidates for publication in scholarly journals. Peer review is in effect a form of quality control conducted by those with authority on the topic. Along with recognizing physical differences between scholarly journals and "popular" sources, understanding the purpose and process of peer review has been a traditional approach to one-shot instruction requests that focus on source evaluation. This approach offers a definitive and dichotomous strategy that can be accomplished in fifty minutes. As librarians, this strategy has served us fairly well. As far as the students go, however, what do they learn? Most likely: "I need to use peer-reviewed sources for my assignments because they are reliable"; "a peer-reviewed source is credible because it was written by someone with a PhD"; "I can check a box in the database or use Google Scholar to find what I need"; "peer-reviewed sources are always the best sources," and so on. These takeaways are not *bad*. However, they tend to oversimplify the purpose and process of peer review. In addition, while the aforesaid approach is possibly sufficient for first-year courses, upper-level students would benefit from a more critical discussion of scholarly peer review. In this lesson, undergraduates will learn about the purpose of peer review by comparing the type of peer review they do in their writing courses to scholarly peer review, and will role-play the different characters in the process who often get little attention during sessions on peer review and source evaluation, including editors and peer reviewers.

LEARNING OUTCOME

The students will learn what peer review means within the world of scholarly research and will survey various parts of the peer-review process in order to understand both the purpose and the process of peer review.

PREPARATION

Create a slide presentation with one slide for each of the following questions:

- Have you taken part in peer review? If so, could you explain when and how?
- What is the purpose of this type of peer review?
- Describe the steps that you've taken when doing peer review.

Note that the questions involve students explaining how they have peer-reviewed writing by their classmates, likely during a writing course. This serves as a jumping-off point for a discussion about the scholarly peer-review process. If you know that a particular group of students has not peer-reviewed writing, you may want to skip this introduction.

You will need one "Peer-Review Process Roles" worksheet (worksheet 1.2) for each group of three to four students. Locate an example of a research article that has yet to be published or that appears to be a draft. A scholarly institutional repository would be a promising place to find this type of article. Make a copy of the article for each group. Choose a peer-reviewed journal that aligns with the aim of the chosen article and that has instructions for authors on its website.

INSTRUCTION

ACTIVITY ONE: PURPOSE OF PEER REVIEW

Class discussion, 15 to 20 minutes

Display and discuss with students the questions on the pre-prepared slides. Ask if they know of other types of peer review. Guide this discussion towards peer review as it is understood within the scholarly research ecosystem. This may require an explanation of the scholarly conversation, depending on the prior knowledge of the students.

Points to highlight:

- Scholarly conversations can take various forms, but they occur formally through the publication of research studies in peer-reviewed journals.
- Peer review has a distinct meaning in the world of scholarly research.
- Peer review helps to ensure reliability within the scholarly conversation.
- Peer review requires a different publication process than most news and magazine stories that you read online or in print.

Questions to ask:

- Why do scholars, such as researchers and even your own professors, want to publish in peer-reviewed journals?
- What might happen to the credibility of a research study if it is published in a non-peer-reviewed information source rather than a peer-reviewed journal?

ACTIVITY TWO: PROCESS OF PEER REVIEW

Group work, class discussion, 15 to 20 minutes

Explain to the class that because they now have a shared understanding of the *purpose* of peer review in scholarly research, the focus of the session will shift to the *process* of peer review. Take a few minutes to show the students examples of journals' websites. Highlight the "instructions for authors" section and the descriptions of the purpose and scope of the journals. You may want to go one step further and explain that some journals are ranked higher than others, and this can influence where a researcher submits their article. Organize the class into groups of three or four students and assign each group a role to play: researcher, editor, peer-reviewer, or reader. Ask the students to briefly describe what they know about their assigned role in the peer-review process.

It may help to prompt students with a couple of questions:

- How does a journal choose peer-reviewers?
- What is the journal editor's role?

Give each group a copy of the research article that you chose for this activity, along with the "Peer-Review Process Roles" worksheet (worksheet 1.2). Students can use the internet to help them answer the questions.

ASSESSMENT PROMPT

"Sketch or describe your understanding of the peer-review process. This should include both the people and steps involved."

WORKSHEET 1.2

PEER-REVIEW PROCESS ROLES

Discuss and answer the questions related to your group's assigned role in the peer-review process.

RESEARCHERS—GROUP 1

- How would you describe the purpose of your research?
- Do you agree that the chosen journal is an appropriate place to submit your article? Why or why not?

EDITORS—GROUP 2

- What are some things you can look for to determine if the author followed the guidelines and meets the aim of the journal?
- What sort of research do you accept? Does this article align with that?
- Let's assume the article meets your expectations. What do you do now?

PEER-REVIEWERS—GROUP 3

Assume you also conduct research on the topic of the article.

- What are criteria that you will consider that is special to the journal?
- What are some general guidelines to follow as a peer-reviewer (can look online).
- How much time do you have to review the article?

READERS—GROUP 4

Assume you also conduct research on the topic of the article.

- Why do you trust the data and results in this article?
- What are some ways you could use this research in your own research?

LESSON 5

MARKERS OF AUTHORITY

SUMMARY

Students brainstorm the factors that can determine the authority of a scholar and practice applying these factors to a professor they know.

SKILL LEVEL

Intermediate to Advanced

CONTEXT

The concept of authority often serves as the focal point in library instruction sessions on source evaluation. This involves asking students to list the factors that indicate whether a scholar might be considered an authority on a given subject or topic. Referencing the credentials of a scholar (i.e., they attended X school and work at Y university) to confirm their authority usually suffices for undergraduates, yet we know that this fails to consider the full picture. This lesson expands on credentials, introducing students to additional types of information that can be found online and used to judge authority. This should give students an arsenal of markers to consider rather than the usual and solitary "because they have a PhD." Keep in mind that when you ask students to list criteria—for any purpose, not just in this lesson—you risk the chance that they will consider the criteria a "checklist." Checklists require minimal critical thinking and can oversimplify complex ideas. And they often involve yes-or-no answers or quantifiable attributes. Multiple indicators (some quantifiable, some not so much) considered as a whole, however, can strengthen a case for authority, and that is what this lesson attempts to do. The subjective nature of this lesson could be challenging to undergraduates who want definite answers, along with concrete paths to find those answers. By exposing students to ambiguity, however, you help to elevate their critical thinking skills.

LEARNING OUTCOME

The students will explore various types of information available online that can help them to determine the authority of scholars, in order to expand their evaluative skills in this area.

PREPARATION

Each student will need a print or electronic copy of the "My Professor's Authority" worksheet (worksheet 1.3), as well as internet access. Create a list of backup faculty and instructors on your campus who conduct research (or elsewhere if necessary) for those students who need help choosing a professor in Activity Two.

INSTRUCTION

ACTIVITY ONE: IDENTIFYING AUTHORITATIVE ATTRIBUTES

Class discussion, 10 to 15 minutes

Ask students for the reasons why they would search for information about an author of a scholarly article. No doubt, the responses will overwhelmingly include answers along the lines of "to determine the author's authority or credibility." Have students brainstorm the factors that help them do this and why the factors they share matter in relation to authority. It may prove challenging for students to think beyond "because they have a PhD," so be prepared to offer suggestions such as:

- Does the person teach on a specific subject or topic? Do they work at a research university or institution?
- Have they published several articles or books on a specific topic?
- Do they give lectures to other experts on their area of expertise?
- Do other scholars cite their articles or books in their own research?
- Does the person publish in peer-reviewed journals?
- Are they quoted in the news as an authority on a subject?
- Do they serve as the editor of a scholarly journal in their area of expertise?

It would be helpful to write your list of potential attributes on a whiteboard or use a pre-prepared slide, as well as using an example of a scholar to show specific places online where this sort of information can be located.

ACTIVITY TWO: SEARCHING FOR AUTHORITATIVE ATTRIBUTES

Individual work, class discussion, 20 to 25 minutes

Provide each student with a copy of the "My Professor's Authority" worksheet (worksheet 1.3) and explain that they will explore online the authority of a professor of their choosing. After students complete the worksheet, then review with them the factors they listed, jotting down common themes on a whiteboard or large piece of paper. Stress the point that no one factor can determine authority—that they must synthesize the information. If the worksheet proves too difficult, rather than finding the factors themselves, direct students to answer specific questions, such as "Choose one of the scholarly journals that Dr. X published in. What information can you find about this journal? Is it held in high regard? How can you tell? Why would that matter when determining the authority of Dr. X?"

ASSESSMENT PROMPTS

- "What are some factors that when used together can help to confirm the authority of a scholar on a specific subject?"
- "Can one piece of information determine a scholar's authority on a topic? Explain."

WORKSHEET 1.3

MY PROFESSOR'S AUTHORITY

1. Choose one of your professors (past or present) who conducts research and write their name below.

2. What is one subject that they research? You can search online if not sure. Write your answers below.

3. Now search online to see what information you can find about your professor's authority on this subject. List below at least 3 factors that you locate that can help determine the level of authority that your professor has on this subject.

   - Factor One:

   - Factor Two:

   - Factor Three:

4. Based on what you found in Question 3, do you believe your professor is an expert in the subject that you identified in Question 2? Why or why not? Use the factors that you located to support your answer.

LESSON 6

SHARING THE RESULTS

SUMMARY

The students make connections between scholarly dissemination and its role in keeping the scholarly conversation moving forward. They explore various channels in which scholars share their research.

SKILL LEVEL

Intermediate to Advanced

CONTEXT

ACRL's Scholarly Communications Committee, which is responsible for the document "Principles and Strategies for the Reform of Scholarly Communication" (2003), defined scholarly communication as "the system through which research and other scholarly writings are created, evaluated for quality, disseminated to the scholarly community, and preserved for future use. The system includes both formal means of communication, such as publication in peer-reviewed journals, and informal channels, such as electronic listservs."[4]

It may be obvious to you that this definition includes both the dissemination of research and the research process itself. Depending on how you define *communication*, however, scholarly communication *could* be defined as dissemination practices only. This lesson assumes that scenario, emphasizing the methods that are used to share research and ideas within the scholarly community and beyond. When covering this topic with students, you should also consider the connection between scholarly communication and the scholarly conversation. These concepts sustain each other, and due to their interconnected relationship, you may find it challenging to discuss one without the other; that is why the first activity of this lesson offers students a refresher on the scholarly conversation. If students have little or no familiarity with this concept yet have knowledge of peer review in the context of scholarly research, a brief introduction to the concept of scholarly conversation may suffice instead. Regarding the actual communication channels, students need to have an agreed-upon interpretation of the concepts of *formal* and *informal*, or whichever words you choose to describe the range of possible outlets for scholarly dissemination. This is not unlike expecting first-year students to "broaden" or "narrow" a database keyword search, a task which requires a grasp of subjective constructs that may mean a certain thing to us as librarians, but not to undergraduates who have limited searching experience. In this case, *formal* can be defined as long-established structures used to disseminate authoritative research, mostly referring to peer-reviewed journals and professional conferences. Informal channels for scholarly conversations could be described as more inclusive, faster, but possibly less authoritative, such as social media, discussion boards, and blogs. This lesson gives students an opportunity to come to an agreed-upon understanding of the terms *formal* and *informal*, especially as applied to the process of scholarly dissemination.

LEARNING OUTCOME

Students will brainstorm the characteristics of information-sharing methods in order to recognize how the scholarly conversation occurs through various scholarly communication channels.

PREPARATION

Choose the words you plan to use to describe the various types of communication. This lesson uses the terms *formal* and *informal*, but you may have other words that are more relevant to a particular group of undergraduates. Each group of three or four students will need a folder that contains descriptions on separate sheets of paper of everyday communication methods such as text messaging or applications used for texting, social media, talking on the phone, talking in-person, e-mail, and so on. Another set of terms for the folder should focus on the communication methods used by scholars to share their ideas and research, including peer-reviewed articles, e-mail, presentations at professional conferences, scholarly profiles, blogs, videos, and social media. Plan to provide the groups with adhesive appropriate for classroom walls or whiteboards. Lastly, because the term *dissemination* may be new to students, if you choose to use it during the session, be sure to provide a definition in the context of the scholarly research ecosystem.

INSTRUCTION

ACTIVITY ONE: SCHOLARLY CONVERSATION REFRESHER

Class discussion, 10 to 15 minutes

How you choose to begin this discussion will depend on the prior knowledge of a particular group of undergraduates. If they are already familiar with the concept of the scholarly conversation, you might open with:

"We've discussed the purpose of the scholarly conversation, so could someone remind us of what that is?"; or, "If you remember from our prior lessons, the scholarly conversation allows research to advance, it's the communication that occurs between scholars."

Survey the students on ways that the scholarly conversation occurs. If needed, prompt the class with relevant questions:

- By chatting at professional conferences and posting thoughts about their research on social media, are scholars taking part in the scholarly conversation? Explain your answer.
- What role do peer-reviewed articles play in the scholarly conversation?

ACTIVITY TWO: CHANNELS OF DISSEMINATION

Class discussion, group work, 20 to 25 minutes

To connect the scholarly conversation with its dissemination, explain to students that peer-reviewed articles, presentations at professional conferences, and even social media provide the conduit for the scholarly conversation to move forward. Whichever terms that you chose to help organize the various types of dissemination channels, ask students to consider those words. For instance:

- What does the adjective *formal* mean to you?
- When someone says that something is *informal*, what does that mean?

Students will likely choose words such as *proper*, *professional*, *serious*, or "dressed-up" to describe formal, with mostly the opposite responses for *informal*.

Transition to the group activity: "Let's dive a bit deeper into the meanings of these two words, particularly in relation to the ways that scholars communicate with one another. To do that, we're going to begin with a scenario that may be more familiar in your life right now than scholarly communication. In a moment, we'll organize into groups of three. Each group will choose a hobby for which there could possibly be a club. For instance, the chess club, the motorcycle club, or the science club. You'll compromise with your group members to decide on the hobby."

Hand each group one of the pre-prepared folders and explain that as officers of this club, they need to communicate to fellow club members information about an upcoming meeting. Continue to explain that the folders contain various strategies they could choose for communicating this news. Explain further: "Arrange the communication methods on the wall in a row or column, with the first method being what your group believes will be the most informal mode of communication and the last method as the most formal. You'll tape each slip of paper on the wall, from informal to formal communication method."

Next, in a class discussion, ask students to list the characteristics that make these communication methods either more informal or more formal. For instance, what is it about texting that makes it more informal? Answers might include speed, ease, reach, and the possibility of almost instant (and often unedited) replies. Then instruct the class to consider what makes some communication methods more formal than others. Their answers will obviously skew towards the opposite of what they listed for informal communication; however, the importance of accuracy and authority in communication should be introduced if it fails to come up during class discussion. For example:

- Is there a greater chance for mistakes to occur in what you have described as informal or in formal communication? Does this matter for your clubs' communication? Why or why not?
- Do you think club members would be more likely to read a message written and sent by the club president? Explain.
- Now that the class has developed agreed-upon characteristics of formal and informal communication, students will identify what they consider formal and informal communication channels among scholars. Using the second packet of communication methods in the pre-prepared folder, instruct each group to create another scale by taping on the wall what members identify as the most informal means of scholarly communication through to the most formal ones. They should apply the characteristics to justify their choices.

ASSESSMENT PROMPT

"Based on class discussion, explain why peer-reviewed articles could be considered a formal means of scholarly communication."

NOTES

1. Association of College & Research Libraries, *Framework for Information Literacy for Higher Education*, 2015, www.ala.org/acrl/standards/ilframework.
2. Association of College & Research Libraries, *Framework*.
3. Association of College & Research Libraries, *Framework*.
4. Association of College & Research Libraries, Scholarly Communications Committee, "Principles and Strategies for the Reform of Scholarly Communication," 2003, www.ala.org/acrl/publications/whitepapers/principlesstrategies.

CHAPTER 2

PEOPLE

The people who actually conduct research receive only minor attention in traditional library instruction sessions, or in classroom discussions in general, except perhaps in the context of authority. This chapter gives undergraduates a better understanding of the roles and expectations of their professors within the scholarly research ecosystem. The students have an opportunity to consider the diversity of scholars, as well as the potential barriers to inclusive scholarly conversations. Because "it takes a village" to conduct meaningful research, the "Conversation Starters" section at the end of this chapter addresses the importance of graduate students and other support staff to successful research.

LESSON 7

WHAT IS A SCHOLAR?

SUMMARY

Students will brainstorm their own definition of *scholar*, and then work in groups to refine their ideas.

SKILL LEVEL

Novice to Intermediate

CONTEXT

The term *scholar* is fundamental in nature; it serves as the root of words in the research ecosystem such as *scholarly* and *scholarship*. Interestingly, though, the term itself seems a bit antiquated, and perhaps even elitist. For instance, on college campuses, undergraduates refer to faculty members by titles such as *professor* and perhaps *researcher* in certain contexts, but rarely do we hear students refer to a faculty member as a *scholar*. Despite its not being used regularly on a day-to-day basis, Google chose the term *scholar* to name Google Scholar, its massive scholarly index. We all know that Google Scholar has grown extremely popular in the scholarly world, even among undergraduates. Do students infer that *scholars* publish the resources found in Google Scholar, or that *scholars* use the search engine to find scholarly research? Do undergraduates understand the possible implications for scholarly communications because Google chose to use *scholar* in the title? We could go on, but obviously many questions arise from this one simple word—enough so that dedicated class time for students to explore the meaning of the word may prove worthwhile. Although this lesson focuses on the term *scholar*, it can serve as a template lesson for other words within the scholarly research vocabulary.

LEARNING OUTCOME

Students will compare various definitions of *scholar* in order to gain a broad understanding of its meaning.

PREPARATION

Each student will need a copy of the "Definitions of a Scholar" handout (box 2.1). The sources of the definitions used in box 2.1 are the *Cambridge Dictionary*, Google, the *Merriam-Webster*

DEFINITIONS OF A SCHOLAR

Cambridge Dictionary: "a person with great knowledge, usually of a particular subject."

Google: "a specialist in a particular branch of study, especially the humanities; a distinguished academic."

Merriam-Webster Dictionary: "a person who has done advanced study in a special field."

Oxford English Dictionary: "a person who is highly educated and knowledgeable, usually as a result of studying at a university."

Wikipedia: "a person who devotes themselves to scholarly pursuits, particularly to the study of an area in which they have developed expertise."

BOX 2.1 *"Definitions of a Scholar"* handout

Dictionary, the *Oxford English Dictionary*, and *Wikipedia*.[1] You should decide beforehand whether to refer to the words used in the definitions as "descriptors," "characteristics," or something else.

Here are some additional ideas as you prepare:

- Challenge the students to locate definitions rather than providing the definitions for them.
- Emphasize a specific type of scholar. For instance, a lesson on biology scholars may look different than a lesson on history scholars.

INSTRUCTION

ACTIVITY ONE: CHARACTERISTICS OF SCHOLARS

Individual work, 10 to 15 minutes

Ask each student to write a definition of the term *scholar* without help from outside sources. Let the class know that they will return to their definitions later. Next, provide a copy of the "Definitions of a Scholar" handout (box 2.1) to each student and ask them to highlight or circle what they believe to be the most accurate terms or characteristics used to describe a scholar. Make this activity more challenging by limiting the number of words that students can circle.

ACTIVITY TWO: DEFINING SCHOLAR

Group work, class discussion, individual work, 15 to 20 minutes

Building on Activity One, organize the class into groups of three or four. The students in each group will compare among themselves the words they highlighted and agree on the three most important descriptors of a scholar. Encourage them to add relevant words to their lists that they feel are missing from the definitions. After the groups share their words on the whiteboard, refer to their choices of words as you lead students toward the creation of a common definition of *scholar* that is appropriate for the context of the class.

ASSESSMENT PROMPT

Students return to their original definitions of *scholar* written at the start of the lesson and answer the following question: "Are there terms or phrases that you included in your definition of *scholar* that you would change based on our class discussion?"

LESSON 8

PATHS TO A PhD

SUMMARY

Students consider the educational requirements for a variety of familiar professions in order to gain a sense of the type of education required to be a college professor.

SKILL LEVEL

Intermediate to Advanced

CONTEXT

Ask a group of undergraduates why their professors have the authority to teach on a particular topic, and a popular response will no doubt be "because they have a PhD." This credential suggests to students a person who has successfully completed—or endured—many years of schooling. During one-shot library instruction sessions on source evaluation, students rely on "because they have a PhD" as one of a handful of explicit evaluative criteria, particularly for peer-reviewed sources. Students apply this criterion without a thorough comprehension of what earning a PhD involves, though. In order to truly grasp the concept of authority, undergraduates should recognize the type and intensity of training it takes to earn a doctorate. This lesson guides students as they flesh out the general path that their professors took in their pursuit of a doctorate or other terminal degree.

LEARNING OUTCOME

Students will compare the educational requirements of various professions in order to gain perspective on the education needed to be a college professor.

PREPARATION

Each group of three or four students will need a copy of the "Education of Professionals" worksheet (worksheet 2.1), access to a whiteboard or easel pad, dry-erase markers, and internet access. For Activity One, choose four professions that require a college degree in order to practice. A couple of your choices should require additional degrees; for example, an architect, high school teacher, attorney, or general practitioner. Complete an example sketch for the "Education of Professionals" worksheet to share with students before they complete the worksheet on their own. In addition to text, consider drawing objects on the sketch (e.g., a mortarboard to signify graduation) to help encourage their creativity and interest in the activity. The ease or difficulty of this activity will depend on whether you allow students to search online for help in answering the questions on the worksheet. If you choose to allow students to search online, note that they will probably pull from the online *Occupational Outlook Handbook* for both activities, so check to ensure that its information aligns with the purpose of your lesson.[2] Note that this lesson could center around other professions that play a role in scholarly research, such as full-time researchers, lab assistants, or grant writers. Choose ones with the most relevance to your specific group of undergraduates.

INSTRUCTION

ACTIVITY ONE: EDUCATION OF PROFESSIONALS

Group work, class discussion, 15 to 20 minutes

Share your example sketch for the "Education of Professionals" worksheet and lead a brief discussion about it. Next, organize the students into groups of three or four. Assign each group one of the pre-chosen professions and ask them to follow the directions on the "Education of Professionals" worksheet (worksheet 2.1). The multitude of paths and specialties for each profession means it may be difficult to determine one set of correct answers for this activity. You should be able to judge, however, if students have a reasonable idea of each educational path.

Lead a discussion about each group's sketch. Discussion questions:

- Why does the amount of education and training needed vary among these professions?
- Why do some of these careers require professional licensing?
- Does one's college major matter in all of these professions? Explain.
- How are the educational paths different than you envisioned?

ACTIVITY TWO: EDUCATION OF COLLEGE PROFESSORS

Group work, class discussion, 15 to 20 minutes

Alongside the first sketch, groups will duplicate the activity just completed but will consider *college professor* as the career. Because of the broadness of this term, consider assigning the groups specific disciplines (e.g., chemistry professor, history professor, engineering professor, biology professor). To aid with inclusivity, assign each group a specific university or college to investigate. For instance, what does "X University" require for a doctorate in chemistry? When finished, review each group's sketch with the class. Encourage the students to think critically about the sketches. Discussion questions:

- Does a doctorate require students to take courses in how to conduct research, such as research methods? If so, why?
- What major similarities and differences in education and training do you recognize between the various disciplines?
- How do these sketches of professors compare to the professions that you researched for the first sketch? Do the professors require a similar level of expertise to work in their respective fields?
- Who has more authority to teach a business class, someone with a PhD in business management or the CEO of a Fortune 500 company?

ASSESSMENT PROMPTS

- "List three new facts you learned today about the process of earning a PhD."
- "Choose a profession from Activity One you believe has similar requirements to a PhD and explain the similarities and differences between the requirements."

WORKSHEET 2.1

EDUCATION OF PROFESSIONALS

On the whiteboard, sketch out the educational path of your assigned career. Use different colored markers, text, and/or drawings to help visualize the path. Questions to consider for each path:

a. What should someone on this professional track major in? What degrees do they need?

b. What type of college or university must they attend?

c. What internships or apprenticeships are required before they can obtain their degree?

d. How many years does it take before someone can practice in the profession?

e. How is the educational path different than you envisioned?

LESSON 9

DIVERSITY AMONG SCHOLARS

SUMMARY

The students both describe in writing and visualize their understanding of a scholar. The visualizations should provide students with a greater awareness of potential biases or stereotypes they may hold, as well as emphasize the presence of diversity within the world of scholarly research.

SKILL LEVEL

Novice to Intermediate

CONTEXT

If you asked a high school student to visualize someone who spent their days doing research, chances are they would describe someone dressed in a white lab coat. Due to various social and cultural influences, undergraduates can enter college with limited or predisposed ideas about scholars and research. This lesson works to counteract those types of ingrained stereotypes. It encourages a conversation about diversity at a deceptively superficial level—that of physical appearance. In actuality, this strategy serves as an unthreatening conversation-starter with students about recognizing their own potential biases. Note that the visualization activity could also be used to initiate a conversation about the role of women and people of color in the scholarly research ecosystem.

LEARNING OUTCOME

Students will reflect upon their perceptions and assumptions of the characteristics of scholars in order to recognize the diversity of scholars and their work.

PREPARATION

Prioritize the aspects of diversity that you want to emphasize. For example, should you steer the conversation towards gender, race, nationality, education level, type of work, place of work, a combination of these, or does it even matter in the context of the assignment or coursework? Each student will need a blank piece of paper.

INSTRUCTION

⌔ ACTIVITY ONE: CHARACTERISTICS OF SCHOLARS

Individual work, 5 to 10 minutes

Ask each student to write on a blank piece of paper a response to a prompt such as "describe the characteristics of a scholar" or "describe a scholar and their work environment." A more familiar descriptor such as *researcher* may work better than *scholar*, depending on the class. Keep the prompt general in order to allow for a broad interpretation from students. Provide a brief discussion time in which students can share with each other some of the characteristics that they wrote down.

⌔ ACTIVITY TWO: VISUALIZATION OF SCHOLARS

Individual work, class discussion, 20 to 25 minutes

Ask students to put their work to the side and envision a scholar. They may close their eyes if it helps. Explain to the students that the scholar may appear clear and exact or could be a bit fuzzy. Continue to help the students sharpen and refine their image silently by prompting them with questions, such as:

- What is the scholar wearing? A cap and gown, a white lab coat, jeans and a T-shirt, steel-toed boots, a wide-brimmed hat, something else?
- What is the scholar holding? A clipboard, a pair of binoculars, a laptop, a test tube, a shovel, or something else?
- Where is the scholar located? A messy office, a college classroom, an experimental lab, a boat in the ocean, the desert, or somewhere else?
- What is the scholar doing? Reading, teaching, calculating figures, collecting water samples, digging in the dirt, or doing something else?
- What qualifications make this person a scholar? They have a PhD, they have relevant experience, they serve as a university faculty member, or something else?
- Who is with the scholar? Other scholars, graduate students, undergraduate students, community members, or someone else?
- Is the scholar of a particular gender or race? What language do they speak?

Direct the students to then turn to the person next to them and describe the scholar that they imagined. After two minutes of discussion, ask the class if any of the pairs had visualized the exact same scholar. If the students answer "no," have them give reasons why everyone visualized something different. If students answer "yes," ask them to provide the reasons that may have led them to imagine the same type of scholar. Both answers should present an opportunity to address stereotypes (e.g., a scholar is a male wearing a white coat conducting experiments in a lab) and illustrate the breadth and diversity present within the world of scholars.

Here are some questions to aid in discussion:

- How might social media influence how you visualize scholars?
- What sorts of research do news and information outlets report on? Do you recognize biases in their coverage? Explain.
- Could your major or field of study affect your understanding of scholars? Explain.
- Does the college or university you attend shape your concept of research? Why or why not?
- How might current politics or culture influence your thoughts on scholars and their research?
- Do personal beliefs sway your vision of scholars? If so, in what ways?
- How might your educational experiences prior to college affect your understanding of scholars?
- What movies, TV shows, or other forms of entertainment serve as good models for the diversity of scholars and their research, and which ones don't? Explain your choices.
- Are there specific types of research that you associate with a particular gender, race, or nationality? If so, why do you make these associations?

This topic and these questions have the potential to touch on sensitive topics related to the individual backgrounds of students. If this is a problem, try to phrase questions in a less personal way, such as "How might social media influence how a person visualizes scholars?"

ASSESSMENT PROMPT

"Revise your answer to the question in the first activity based on any new information that you learned today, with an emphasis on the qualities of a scholar that contribute to diversity."

LESSON 10

COMMUNITY-GRANTED AUTHORITY

SUMMARY

The students brainstorm an activity or topic in which they have expertise and consider the reasons why they may or may not be an authority in that area. Then they apply these ideas to explore how someone gains authority in a profession, particularly through community.

SKILL LEVEL

Intermediate to Advanced

CONTEXT

As we introduce undergraduates to the world of scholarly research, the scholars who conduct and share their research tend to manifest for students as a monolithic group of individuals who have "credentials" to write within a discipline or on a particular topic. In a library instruction session on source evaluation, a discussion of credentials usually goes hand-in-hand with a discussion of authority. In fact, the inspiration for this lesson, the "Authority Is Constructed and Contextual" frame in the *Framework for Information Literacy for Higher Education*, states that "novice learners may need to rely on basic indicators of authority such as type of publication and author's credentials."[3] Unfortunately, this oversimplification can persist throughout the college career of an undergraduate. Therefore, this lesson tries to challenge novice users to expand upon those indicators of authority by introducing the concept of community, and how discrete communities can bestow "authority" on a person, scholar, or expert for their own distinctive reasons.

LEARNING OUTCOME

Students will explore the differences in meaning between *expertise* and *authority* in order to understand the significance of community-granted authority.

PREPARATION

Each student will need a note card, and each group of three or four students will need a "Gaining Authority" worksheet (worksheet 2.2). Prepare to explain the concept of "community" in this context; that is, a body of people who have expertise in a particular area or field.

Here are some additional ideas as you prepare:

- Tailor the examples on the "Gaining Authority" worksheet to align with the knowledge and experiences of the students.
- Focus the worksheet on different types of professions related to scholarly research.

INSTRUCTION

ACTIVITY ONE: GAINING EXPERTISE

Individual work, class discussion, 20 to 25 minutes

On a whiteboard or presentation slide, display the following questions. Ask each student to anonymously answer the questions on a note card:

- What is something that you know a lot about (e.g., football, algebra, baking)?
- How did you learn what you know about this topic or activity? (For example, formal classes, watching someone else, self-taught from YouTube videos, taking part in the activity?)
- How often do you practice this activity or learn more about it?
- Would you consider yourself an expert on it? Should other people trust your expertise? Why or why not?

Take up the note cards, shuffle them, and then hand them back out. Ask for a few volunteers to read out loud the responses on the note cards. This could lead to a spirited discussion among students about their interests, hobbies, and talents. Guide the class to a conversation about *expertise* and *authority*. Here are some discussion questions:

- Based on what your classmates wrote on the note cards, as well as our discussion, what does it take to be an expert on a topic, activity, or other skill? The possible responses could include education, training, and practice.
- Is being an expert the same as having authority on a topic? Who decides that you are an authority on a topic or activity?

Encourage students to consider the distinctions between *expertise* and *authority* and why the distinction matters.

Providing definitions for the class may be helpful: the *Merriam-Webster Dictionary* says that an expert is "one with the special skill or knowledge representing mastery of a particular subject,"[4] while an authority is "an individual cited or appealed to as an expert."[5]

ACTIVITY TWO: GAINING AUTHORITY

Class discussion, group work, 15 to 20 minutes

Continue the discussion about experts and authorities. Explain that an expert becomes an authority only after other people with expertise in that area acknowledge them as an authority. In other words, an expert gains authority by earning credibility within a particular community. For instance, you could share the following scenario (or some other scenario more relevant to the group of undergraduates in the session):

"A bakery shop owner with twenty years of baking experience and national awards for their apple pie recipe hosts local classes to share their expertise with other apple pie bakers. By paying the fee to attend these classes, it seems that the local community of apple pie bakers has granted authority to the baker based on their years of experience and multiple baking awards."

Organize the students into groups of two or three and give a "Gaining Authority" (worksheet 2.2) worksheet to each group.

After students have completed the worksheet, start a conversation about potential answers to the questions. Possible responses include:

- Kindergarten teachers have *expertise* in early childhood education; they may have gained this expertise through formal education, student-teacher training, many years of on-the-job experience, or continuing professional development. They can build *authority* among their fellow teachers, the parents of their students, and the students themselves, particularly as they get older.
- Electricians have *expertise* in installing and repairing electrical systems; they may have gained the expertise through education at a vocational school, through an apprenticeship, or through studying for a license. They can build *authority* among their fellow electricians and satisfied customers.
- The responses for a scholar could vary greatly, but the *expertise* of a scholar with formal training would most likely come from education, teaching, research, and writing within a focused area of study. A scholar could derive *authority* from students and fellow scholars in that particular area of study as well.

ASSESSMENT PROMPT

"Can you have expertise on a topic and still not be considered an authority? Can you be an authority on a topic and still not be considered to have expertise? Explain both answers."

WORKSHEET 2.2

GAINING AUTHORITY

Answer the following questions based on the ideas we discussed in class today.

a. Consider a recently retired kindergarten teacher. What might they be an expert in? How did they get that expertise?

   What communities might consider the teacher an authority on early childhood education?

b. Think about a newly licensed electrician. What expertise do they have that qualifies them to install electrical wires in a new home? How did they get this expertise?

   In what communities might this electrician gain authority?

c. Choose one of your current or former professors. What sort of expertise does that professor have that makes them qualified to teach a course? How did they get their expertise?

   In what communities might they have authority?

LESSON 11

USES FOR SCHOLARLY PROFILES

SUMMARY

The students learn about online scholarly profiles and brainstorm important uses of this information in the context of scholarly research.

SKILL LEVEL

Advanced

CONTEXT

Many scholars carefully curate their online scholarly profiles. This attention to detail can benefit a scholar when hiring and tenure decisions come around. In the earlier days of the internet, before the introduction of sophisticated online aggregators, scholars created websites to showcase their research and other accomplishments. Although university departmental websites still maintain pages dedicated to faculty publications and research interests, we now have more options for where to locate this type of information. Today, powerful automated systems can pull together this information with minimal human intervention, collecting links to publications and calculating relevant metrics that are useful to students, scholars, hiring committees, granting agencies, and so on. Various types of these sites exist. Google Scholar's scholarly profiles were chosen as the example in this lesson due to that search engine's wide acceptance in the scholarly community, the variety of metrics that it offers, and its brand familiarity among students. As a disclaimer, however, no system is perfect, and this includes Google Scholar. If it can be done without overwhelming the students, consider adding ORCID with its educational background section and publication lists, or Web of Science with its citation counts, as additional examples.

LEARNING OUTCOME

Students explore the information available on Google Scholar's scholarly profiles in order to consider the reasons why this information could be useful to them or to other scholars.

PREPARATION

Each group of three or four students will need a copy of the "Scholarly Profile" worksheet (worksheet 2.3). To frame this worksheet as a real-world scenario, choose an active and up-to-date Google Scholar profile for each group of students, or one example to be used by all of the groups. For either option, match the portion of the scenario from the worksheet "and are considered expert scholars in (X) field of study" to the field of study or expertise of the chosen scholar.

INSTRUCTION

ACTIVITY ONE: INTRODUCTION TO SCHOLARLY PROFILES

Class discussion, 15 to 20 minutes

Depending on the particular group of undergraduates, you may need to succinctly explain the purpose of Google Scholar; and for any group of undergraduates, explain that in addition to lists of citations to scholarly articles, Google Scholar gathers information about the scholars who conduct the research. Display to the class an example of a Google Scholar profile and review the types of information available in it. The different types of information might include place of employment, areas of research interest and expertise, number of citations, number of publications, years of publications, links to additional information, coauthors, and Google Scholar metrics' attempts to measure the impact of the scholar's research. Let students know that you will not be digging deep into the metrics, but you could give a brief overview of their function. Here are some possible discussion questions:

- Why do you think Google Scholar collects this information?
- How might you use this information as a student?

ACTIVITY TWO: DIGGING DEEPER INTO SCHOLARLY PROFILES

Group work, 15 to 20 minutes

The students next pair up to complete the "Scholarly Profile" worksheet (worksheet 2.3). Without prior instruction on the topic, the prompt on the worksheet could prove difficult for undergraduates. You always have the option of completing the worksheet with them, guiding students toward responses such as "potential research collaborations" and "critical hiring decisions" as reasons why researchers or faculty members might use the information available in a scholarly profile. Make the point that these reasons can be important for both job stability and career advancement.

ASSESSMENT PROMPTS

- "How might you use scholarly profiles in your future research projects?"
- "Suppose one of your professors is unfamiliar with scholarly profiles. How would you convince them of their usefulness?"

PEOPLE   41

WORKSHEET 2.3

SCHOLARLY PROFILE

You and your partner are researchers, faculty members, and professors at (X) university, and are considered expert scholars in (X) field of study. Choose three pieces of information available about (X) scholar on their Google Scholar profile and consider how you might use this information.

1. Information type:

   How might you use this information in your roles as scholars, researchers, faculty members, and/or professors?

2. Information type:

   How might you use this information in your work as a scholars, researchers, faculty members, and/or professors?

3. Information type:

   How might you use this information in your work as a scholars, researchers, faculty members, and/or professors?

LESSON 12

INCLUSIVITY AND THE SCHOLARLY CONVERSATION

SUMMARY

Students consider the consequences of exclusivity in real-world situations and transfer that knowledge to learn about the barriers to inclusivity within the scholarly conversation.

SKILL LEVEL

Intermediate to Advanced

CONTEXT

The "Scholarship as Conversation" frame of the *Framework for Information Literacy for Higher Education* describes the problem of exclusivity that exists within the scholarly research ecosystem:

"While novice learners and experts at all levels can take part in the conversation, established power and authority structures may influence their ability to participate and can privilege certain voices and information."[6]

This lesson takes on the issue. While undergraduates may have seen or experienced for themselves exclusion in their own lives based on gender, race, economic background, or something else, the notion that it pervades scholarly research will likely be new to them. If you choose to use words directly from the *Framework*, for example, *novice learners*, *experts*, *established power and authority structures*, and *privilege*, you will need to give students space to understand and process these concepts in the context of scholarly research. Even the term *voice* as used in the *Framework* and in this lesson should be addressed upfront as a representation or even a metaphor for the various ways a scholar shares their ideas and research—not a literal voice, but rather a figurative one. Lastly, for this lesson to make sense to them, students will need some exposure to the concept of the scholarly conversation and peer review.

LEARNING OUTCOME

Students will consider that the scholarly conversation may not represent all relevant voices, in order to recognize that certain perspectives could be missing.

PREPARATION

Create a few examples for the first activity of exclusive situations that would be familiar to the students. Also, each group of three to four students will require a "Barriers to Inclusivity" worksheet (worksheet 2.4). This activity could also be paperless, where students enter their responses in an online form that feeds into a spreadsheet. You can then display the anonymous responses for the class to review and discuss.

Here are some additional ideas to consider as you prepare:

- Issues of race, gender, and other biases may come up during this activity. You could encourage students to share an experience in which they felt excluded. However, due to the sensitive nature of the topic, having established a safe space for the students to share their thoughts and ideas prior to this lesson is ideal.
- In this lesson, the term *exclusivity* will most likely result in a negative connotation for students. You should consider beforehand whether to share positive examples of exclusivity in order to give students a more balanced impression of the concept.

INSTRUCTION

ACTIVITY ONE: EXCLUSIVITY

Class discussion, 15 to 20 minutes

Ask students to first define the term *exclusive*, which may be more familiar to them than the term *inclusive*. To help encourage discussion, give the class a couple of real-world examples such as an "exclusive party" or an "exclusive sneak peek" of a movie. They should recognize that *exclusive*—at least in relation to these examples—means that only certain people would attend an event or be "in" on something. Stated another way, some people are left out or not invited. You can build on this point with additional scenarios that should be relatable to most undergraduates:

- "All except one child receive an invitation to a classmates' birthday party. Describe the potential outcomes for this child and the other children in the class to an exclusive birthday party."
- "A college rejects any application from a potential student with a high school GPA below 3.5. What are some outcomes of such an exclusive college admission process?"
- "Your professor offers a study group for students who have a grade of C or lower at midterm. What are your thoughts on excluding students with higher grades from the study group?"

The students should recognize that exclusivity often results in hurt feelings or more serious outcomes, such as discrimination.

ACTIVITY TWO: INCLUSIVITY IN RESEARCH

Class discussion, 20 to 25 minutes

Now that students have defined the word *exclusive*, ask them to consider the opposite and define *inclusive*. This should be a fairly straightforward task after the discussion in the first activity. Turn the focus to scholarly research and ask, "Why is it important to have a variety of perspectives in scholarly research?" After students provide their answers, continue with:

"Scholars have conversations in a variety of ways. They communicate at professional conferences, through blog posts and social media, and of course via peer-reviewed articles. In the world of scholarly research, we know that peer-reviewed publication is considered the most authoritative type of communication."

Introduce the next activity, in which students will consider the inclusivity of the scholarly conversation—and more specifically, whether it includes and invites perspectives from all scholars who have expertise to share. Organize the students into groups of three or four to complete the "Barriers to Inclusivity" worksheet (worksheet 2.4). If this activity seems too challenging for students to tackle on their own in groups, you can lead them through the worksheet as a full-class activity. Here are some potential answers to the worksheet questions:

- New researchers might be excluded due to their unawareness of how or where to best share their ideas and research. They could also face a system where new scholars must first "pay their dues" in order to be included.
- Gender and race could exclude people due to entrenched societal discrimination. There are, for example, socioeconomic issues that affect educational opportunities and therefore keep many people from entering college, stereotypes that limit entry into particular fields (e.g., the disproven belief that women cannot excel in STEM fields), and institutions with weak hiring practices for diversity and inclusion.
- While perhaps not seen as much as an issue compared to other kinds of discrimination, older scholars could be seen as not "keeping up" or as old-fashioned in their methods.

To avoid overwhelming students, this lesson does not include the possible solutions to the problems presented, as described in the *Framework*: "Developing familiarity with the sources of evidence, methods, and modes of discourse in the field assists novice learners to enter the conversation. New forms of scholarly and research conversations provide more avenues in which a wide variety of individuals may have a voice in the conversation."[7] These possible solutions could be included as a discussion, or as additional questions on the worksheet, however.

ASSESSMENT PROMPT

"What are some reasons why a particular scholarly conversation may not be considered inclusive?"

WORKSHEET 2.4

BARRIERS TO INCLUSIVITY

Answer the following questions to the best of your ability, without using the internet.

a. Why might a new researcher be excluded from the scholarly conversation?

b. Why might gender influence whether someone is left out of the conversation?

c. Why might people of color have a difficult time joining the scholarly conversation?

d. Why may a retired researcher be excluded from the scholarly conversation?

CONVERSATION STARTERS

GRADUATE STUDENTS

You can use the questions below to lead a conversation with undergraduates about graduate students in a couple of ways. First, you can introduce them to the role that graduate students play at research universities and within the scholarly research ecosystem. Second, you can help undergraduates who may be interested in graduate school learn more about the process and system. For example, although a wealth of information can be found online, opportunities such as graduate assistantships and research expectations should be pointed out to them.

ACTIVITY IDEAS

- Bring in graduate students to speak with undergraduates about the variety of opportunities on campus to take part in research.
- Students with similar disciplinary interests can pair up to investigate graduate schools.

DISCUSSION QUESTIONS

- What are some reasons to obtain a graduate degree?
- Do all colleges and universities offer graduate degrees? What about your university?
- How do graduate students contribute to research on campus? If so, in what ways?
- What are teaching assistantships? What are research assistantships? How can you secure an assistantship?
- Why are some graduate students paid to attend graduate school?
- What are some strategies to secure financial funding as a graduate student?
- What is a graduate fellowship?
- Do graduate students publish their research?
- How does the work of graduate students benefit the university?
- Do graduate students have the same protections and benefits as do full-time employees and faculty?
- What contributions do the students in master's programs make to an institution? What about doctoral students?
- What tests are required to apply for graduate school? How much do they cost?
- What is the role of a graduate faculty advisor? Can you choose your advisor?
- Are there ways to gain scholarly research experience prior to graduate school?

- Are theses and dissertations considered scholarly publications?
- Does obtaining a master's degree guarantee acceptance into a doctoral program?

SUPPORT TEAM

You can help undergraduates to recognize the range of human effort required for scholarly research with these activities and discussion questions. Due to the innumerable situational factors that can arise during a research project, the roles emphasized below are in no way an exhaustive list.

ACTIVITY IDEAS

- Students think through the various types of expertise needed to complete a research study. They brainstorm the offices or people on campus that could fill those needs.
- Assign students a research support role to investigate, and have them report back to their classmates on the possible duties of this role.
- Ask students to consider how discipline-specific factors could influence the type of skills that would be needed on a research project. For instance, a research project in biochemistry, in comparison to a research project in psychology.

DISCUSSION QUESTIONS

- In addition to the researchers or scholars, what other expertise is needed on a research team?
- What is the role of graduate students on a research team? What about undergraduates?
- What are some responsibilities of lab assistants?
- How do librarians and archivists support scholars with their research?
- What role do professional grant writers play within the research process?
- What help do researchers need in organizing and sharing the data that has been gathered?
- How might a trained statistician contribute to a research project?
- What role could a web designer have on a research team? Describe a scenario.
- Do some disciplines require larger research teams than others?
- Who can help a research team choose the most appropriate journals in which to publish their results?
- Are there research projects that can function with only the primary researchers and no support staff? If you answer yes, describe an example scenario. If you answer no, explain why.

NOTES

1. *Cambridge Dictionary*, s.v. "Scholar," https://dictionary.cambridge.org/us/dictionary/english/scholar; Google's English Dictionary by Oxford Languages, s.v. "Scholar"; *Merriam-Webster Dictionary*, s.v. "Scholar," www.merriamwebster.com/dictionary/scholar?utm_campaign=sd&utm_medium=serp&utm_source=jsonld; *Oxford English Dictionary*, s.v. "Scholar"; *Wikipedia*, s.v. "Scholar," https://en.wikipedia.org/wiki/Scholar.
2. U.S. Department of Labor, Bureau of Labor Statistics, *Occupational Outlook Handbook*, www.bls.gov/ooh/.
3. Association of College & Research Libraries, *Framework for Information Literacy for Higher Education*, www.ala.org/acrl/standards/ilframework.
4. *Merriam-Webster Dictionary*, s.v. "Expert," www.merriam-webster.com/dictionary/expert?utm_campaign=sd&utm_medium=serp&utm_source=jsonld.
5. *Merriam-Webster Dictionary*, s.v. "Authority," www.merriam-webster.com/dictionary/authority.
6. Association of College & Research Libraries, *Framework*.
7. Association of College & Research Libraries, *Framework*.

CHAPTER 3

TERMINOLOGY

When presented with a research assignment, undergraduates may find themselves in the thick of a new vocabulary, with little if any foundational instruction. Furthermore, variations in teaching styles and research interests among undergraduate instructors may introduce inconsistencies in word meanings that can confuse students. Those of us who have spent time in higher education can confidently say that some instructors devote adequate class time to the introduction of important terminology related to scholarly research, while others overestimate the knowledge and comprehension that students have about key concepts. The lessons in this chapter offer strategies for a gradual introduction of the specialized vocabulary of scholarly research to undergraduates.

LESSON 13

A LEXICON EXISTS

SUMMARY

Students explore the specialized vocabularies associated with familiar occupations and hobbies. They replicate this exercise with a focus on the language of scholarly research.

SKILL LEVEL

Intermediate to Advanced

CONTEXT

Scholarly journals, paywalls, peer review, human subjects, research design, open access—these words represent a fraction of the terms that make up the scholarly research vocabulary. We use this vocabulary to name, describe, and explain concepts related to the scholarly research ecosystem. Think back to how and when you learned these words and their meanings. Did you take a course that taught you all the words associated with scholarly research, or did you learn them as the need arose? Most people would probably say the latter, and it makes sense—humans tend to make an effort to learn what they need at their point of need. It takes years for those who make research a career to master this specialized lexicon, and in our world of fast change, it can be challenging for even the most seasoned researchers to keep up with the newest terminology in their fields. We know that a solitary lesson will not expose students to all the words in the scholarly research vocabulary, but it *can* familiarize them with the *existence* of this vocabulary. At the least, it should provide a basis for students to build their knowledge upon, and give them a glimpse of what may come in future research courses.

LEARNING OUTCOME

Students will consider the importance of specialized vocabularies in order to understand the need for a scholarly research vocabulary.

PREPARATION

For the "draw from the hat" activity, choose a number of common hobbies and occupations and print each one on a small piece of paper. When possible, the choices should take into account what you know about the students' life experiences and backgrounds, since what may be familiar to one student may not be to another. Examples of occupations could include accountant and cashier, while soccer and gaming might work as relatable hobbies; regardless of your choices, the students should be able to list between five and ten terms associated with each occupation and hobby without searching online. All groups need a whiteboard marker and a regular-sized piece of paper. Lastly, prepare enough small prizes for each student in at least two of the groups.

Here are some additional ideas as you prepare:

- Narrow the focus to occupations *or* hobbies. Using them simultaneously provides a scope that helps students recognize that most everything has its own vocabulary, but this approach may not fit every situation.
- For a fun twist, experiment with occupations and hobbies that most people would know something about, but which might be considered unusual, thrill-seeking, or popular. For example, performing magic for an audience, managing a haunted house, skydiving, or earning millions of dollars as a social media influencer.
- As an alternative to drawing from a hat, allow the students to pick from a list that you provide, or allow them to choose their own occupations or hobbies to explore.
- Transform the first activity from group work to individual work by asking each student to brainstorm all of the words associated with one of their own hobbies.
- Allow students to use the internet to help with their brainstorming, knowing however, that the groups will most likely use the same first few search results. If this is problematic, provide specific guidelines for their search that would help alleviate this issue. For example, assign each group a different website.

INSTRUCTION

ACTIVITY ONE: THE VOCABULARIES OF OCCUPATIONS AND HOBBIES

Group work, class discussion, 15 to 20 minutes

Form groups of three or four students each. Assign each group a space at the whiteboard and a name or number. Ask a member of each group to pull a piece of paper out of the hat or bowl.

Instruct the groups to write the occupation or hobby printed on their piece of paper as well as their group's name on the board, and then explain to them the rules of the competition:

"You have two minutes to answer this question: 'What terms and concepts must you understand well to excel at this occupation or hobby?' Without using the internet, brainstorm as many terms and concepts as you can think of and write those on the board. After two minutes, each group will move to the adjacent group's space on the board and will have one minute to add additional words associated with that occupation or hobby. Draw a big circle around your group's added words and include the group name. The rotation will continue until you return to your original place at the board. The group to write the most relevant words wins a prize!"

After students complete the activity, add up the number of words for each group and write the results on the board. Be prepared for the possibility of irrelevant terms and concepts, as well as a tie between groups. Award the prizes, and then lead a discussion about what they wrote.

Here are some discussion questions:

- Were you already familiar with some of these terms? If so, which ones?
- Were some of these vocabularies easier than others to brainstorm? Why or why not?
- Can you think of other occupations and hobbies that would *not* have their own vocabulary?
- Is it essential to understand all the terms associated with an occupation or hobby to be successful at it? Why or why not?

ACTIVITY TWO: THE VOCABULARY OF SCHOLARLY RESEARCH

Group work, class discussion, 20 to 25 minutes

Repeat the exercise, but this time all groups brainstorm words associated with the concept of scholarly research. Rather than writing responses on the board, which could result in students simply scanning the room and copying the responses of other groups, have them write on pieces of paper. When the groups have made their rounds, ask each group to read off their list. Without the use of the internet, the list may be limited, but through discussion you could have students think of more terms. Examples of advanced terms could be *methodology, open access, variables, abstract, quantitative, qualitative, literature review, refereed, theory, reliability, validity, white paper, academic, induction,* and *archives.*

Here are some discussion questions:

- Did you find this list easier, more difficult, or about the same to make than the lists of occupations and hobbies? Why do you think this is the case?
- Do you believe there may be other words associated with scholarly research that you are not aware of? If so, how and when might you learn more terms and concepts related to scholarly research?
- What are some of the benefits to scholarly research if scholars have a standard vocabulary that they use to describe concepts when communicating with each other?

ASSESSMENT PROMPT

"Imagine that two scholars are collaborating to conduct a valid research study. Describe at least one potential consequence to the study if the scholars have different understandings of the term *validity.*"

LESSON 14

STAY CALM AND CHOOSE THE RIGHT WORDS

SUMMARY

In this lesson, students reflect upon a word familiar to them, its relationship and connection to closely related words, and why differences in their meanings matter. The students will apply the same approach in the second activity, but with a focus on a term from the scholarly research vocabulary.

SKILL LEVEL

Intermediate to Advanced

CONTEXT

The terminology that we use when teaching students about scholarly research conversations is not always clear. As an example, undergraduate students inevitably need instruction on source evaluation at some point in their college careers, typically prompted by an assignment that requires the use of certain types of information sources. Examples of terms chosen by instructors to describe the types of sources they expect students to engage with include *credible*, *reliable*, *valid*, *trustworthy*, *authoritative*, *peer-reviewed*, *professional*, and so on; and at times we (librarians, faculty, instructors, students) use these words interchangeably. But is a *credible* source the same as a *reliable* source? A quick search of various dictionaries would reveal similarities in the modern usage of these terms, but clear differences as well. In addition, we rarely expect undergraduates to evaluate the "methods" section of scholarly articles for validity, so what *do* we mean when we ask them to integrate *valid* sources into their writing? This inflation of word meaning may not seem all that significant in these classroom scenarios, but it could prove consequential in the high-stakes world of scholarly research. This lesson—which encourages undergraduates to think critically about the language they use when talking about scholarly research—focuses on the word *scholar* but could apply to most terms in the scholarly research vocabulary.

LEARNING OUTCOME

The students will reflect on the consequences of inaccurate word choices in order to recognize the importance of word choice when conducting scholarly research.

PREPARATION

Choose a word in the scholarly research vocabulary that is relevant to the course or a specific group of students, as well as an example word with which most students are familiar. This lesson will focus on the terms *scholar* and *athlete*, respectively. Prepare one copy of both sets of words listed below for each group of three or four students (one word per piece of paper):

- Set one: scholar, academic, practitioner, historian, professor, social scientist, researcher, scientist, intellectual
- Set two: athlete, Olympian speed skater, gold medalist, gymnast, softball pitcher, competitor

The groups also need access to a whiteboard or large piece of blank paper, adhesive appropriate for whiteboards, dry-erase markers, and internet access. Make an extra set of the athlete-related words for yourself.

INSTRUCTION

ACTIVITY ONE: TERMS USED TO DESCRIBE ATHLETES

Group work, class discussion, 15 to 20 minutes

Prior to class, tape your set of athlete-related words to a whiteboard in a random design. Organize the class into groups of three or four and ask each group to also tape their athlete-related terms to the whiteboard in whatever design they choose. Explain the activity:

"Later in the class, we'll discuss the meaning of the term *scholar*, along with related words and words with similar meanings. We'll do that in order for you to see how sometimes we choose words that we may feel are close enough in meaning, but don't quite fit the situation. If this seems fuzzy right now, no worries. We'll start with a word that most of you should know something about—*athlete*. All the words you've taped on the whiteboard could possibly be used to describe an athlete. I'd like for you to draw either a solid arrow or a dashed arrow between the words to indicate connections and relationships. For example, are all athletes Olympians? No, but some are. So, you'll draw a dashed arrow from athletes to Olympians. What about the reverse? Are all Olympians athletes? Probably, yes; therefore, draw a solid arrow from Olympian to athlete. Indicate these relationships between all of the words, not just *athlete*. For instance, are all gymnasts competitors? Not necessarily, so draw a dashed arrow from gymnast to competitor. Are all competitors gymnasts? No. So you'll draw a dashed arrow from competitors to gymnasts. The goal is to visualize as many relationships between the words as possible." As you explain these examples, draw the appropriate arrows between your set of words to help model the activity.

Although all of the groups may produce slightly different schemas, figure 3.1 offers an example of how one might look. If this activity seems too challenging without a model for

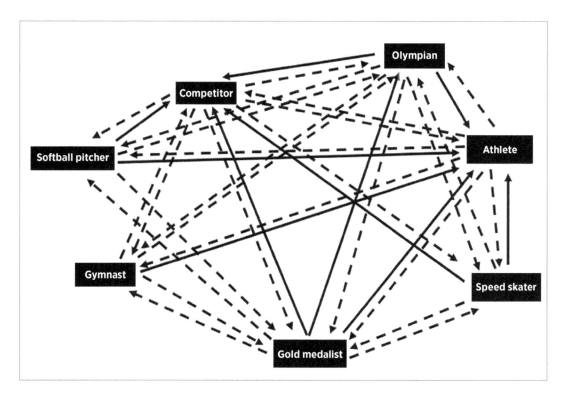

FIGURE 3.1 Athlete: Similar and Related Words example

students to work from, prepare an example before class on a different topic and make a copy for each group.

After the students complete the activity, lead a discussion in which the groups explain the reasoning for how they organized the words. In the absence of just one correct organizational scheme, the exercise could end with a degree of ambiguity. Regardless, students should begin to identify the problems with inaccurate word choice.

ACTIVITY TWO: TERMS USED TO DESCRIBE SCHOLARS

Group work, class discussion, 15 to 20 minutes

Have students duplicate Activity One using the set of words related to *scholars*. This may prove more challenging than the first activity, so allow them to use the internet to define unfamiliar terms. Give each group time to describe why they displayed the words as they did. It may be helpful to prompt the students with discussion questions.

Here are some questions you might use:

- Are all scholars considered academics? Explain.
- Are the terms *scholar* and *researcher* synonymous? Explain.

- How are scholars and practitioners different? How are they the same?
- Is a scientist a scholar? Is a scholar a scientist? Why or why not?
- Do scholars and researchers have the same educational background?

ASSESSMENT PROMPT

"Describe at least one problem that could occur by using the words *peer-reviewed* and *scholarly* interchangeably."

LESSON 15

SCHOLARLY: EXPLORING A FUNDAMENTAL TERM

SUMMARY

The students brainstorm their own definitions of *scholarly,* then reflect on the various ways that their instructors might define *scholarly*. This is achieved through the use of a continuum.

SKILL LEVEL

Novice to Intermediate

CONTEXT

In the course of helping undergraduates locate scholarly sources for their assignments, you may observe that while one instructor will define scholarly sources as anything *credible* or *authoritative*, another will apply the moniker *scholarly* to peer-reviewed sources only. While the latter scenario makes life easier, it also tends to oversimplify source evaluation. This discrepancy is particularly prevalent in first-year writing courses. Therefore, undergraduates may see fluidity from course to course regarding what constitutes a scholarly source. In this lesson, students will investigate definitions of *scholarly* and explore the possible consequences that can result from varied interpretations of the word. This lesson will prove relevant to students at various stages of their college career; they should leave the session empowered to seek clarification from their professors when presented with vague meanings of *scholarly*.

LEARNING OUTCOME

Students will deconstruct the meaning of *scholarly* in order to recognize that academia lacks a standard definition for the term, and why this matters.

PREPARATION

To prepare, create a free-form survey using an audience-response tool with the prompt "What is a scholarly source?" or "Describe a scholarly source." If internet access is unavailable, use note cards in place of the online survey. Select entries for *scholarly* from two or three dictionaries and prepare them for presentation on a screen. Lastly, choose a commonly used word for the continuum example in the second activity.

INSTRUCTION

ACTIVITY ONE: DEFINING "SCHOLARLY"

Individual work, class discussion, 15 to 20 minutes

Begin with students answering the question "What is a scholarly source?" using the online response system. The answers should display in real time on the screen. Take a few minutes to review their responses, and direct the students to identify common words and themes within the answers. As students call them out, choose a volunteer to write those words and themes on the whiteboard. Next, focus on the term *scholarly* by displaying two or three definitions of the word on the screen and give students time to read through them. Examples include the following ones:

- *Merriam-Webster Dictionary* defines *scholarly* as "of, characteristic of, or suitable to learned persons."[1]
- *Oxford English Dictionary* defines *scholarly* as "relating to, or characterizing, a scholar or scholars; befitting, or natural to, a scholar; involving or concerned with research, education, and scholarship; academic, intellectual."[2]
- Google defines *scholarly* as "involving or relating to serious academic study."[3]

Select another student to circle the words written on the whiteboard during the previous exercise that match with the terms and concepts found in the definitions displayed on the screen. Survey the class to see if they would like to add any terms or concepts from the definitions that seem to be missing from their list. Let the students know that they will come back to this list later.

ACTIVITY TWO: THE SCHOLARLY CONTINUUM

Group work, class discussion, 20 to 25 minutes

Lead a brief discussion about the lack of a standard definition of *scholarly*. Possible prompts include:

- Do you know if your instructors use similar definitions of a "scholarly" source? If not, how could you find out?
- What is the most common way you have heard instructors define *scholarly*?

Refer back to the list of words on the whiteboard and explain that instructors may use a variety of these words to describe a scholarly source, and they may even have varying understandings of the descriptors themselves. To help illustrate this point, the class will consider a word that may be more familiar to them than *scholarly*. Draw a blank continuum on the board, using the word you chose prior to the session. The continuum in figure 3.2 uses *happiness* as the class example. Ask students to brainstorm terms that can be used to express the concept of happiness. They are likely to call out words such as *contentment, bliss, joy, cheerfulness, gladness, pleasure,* and *delight*. Students may also use culturally significant terms as well as generational slang. With a marker, write each response on a separate piece of paper. Next, the students will direct you (or volunteers) to tape these words on the continuum based on their perception of the words' meaning. For instance, words that express extreme happiness will be placed on one end of the continuum, while words that express a mild or subdued form of happiness will be taped on the other end. Because of the subjectivity of this activity, the placement of the words may result in a debate among students. When this happens, point out how their varied interpretations of *happiness* can be applied to the concept of *scholarly* as well.

Organize the students in groups of two or three. Draw the "Scholarly Continuum" (figure 3.3) on the whiteboard and ask each group to do the same. Instruct each group to use the words circled on the board to create a continuum for the concept of *scholarly*. Each continuum created will likely be unique, so ask each group to justify their choices. In the absence of a whiteboard, provide students with pieces of paper on which they can write the words and tape them to the wall. This alternative approach also allows students to move the sheets around quickly as they work rather than erasing and rewriting words, and may encourage more participation from all students.

Next, ask the students to compare a few of the words. For instance, do *credible* and *peer-reviewed* mean the same thing? What about a *research* article and an *academic* article? Explain that the closer the words sit on the continuum, the closer they should be in meaning. Therefore, when a writing instructor asks them to use credible sources, this does not necessarily mean that those sources should be peer-reviewed. At this point, encourage the students to clarify their expectations with their professor when faced with this sort of situation, reminding them that any two of their instructors could possibly have differing definitions for *scholarly*.

ASSESSMENT PROMPT

"How might the lack of a standard definition or description of *scholarly* affect you?"

FIGURE 3.2 **Happiness Continuum**

FIGURE 3.3 **Scholarly Continuum**

LESSON 16

IS IT A *SEARCH* OR IS IT *RESEARCH*?

SUMMARY

The students review words used to describe research, specifically *search* and *inquiry*. They apply these two words to research scenarios in order to understand the differences between them and why these distinctions matter.

SKILL LEVEL

Novice to Intermediate

CONTEXT

Undergraduates have most likely used the internet to find information for as long as they can remember, yet the chances are that their approach has involved more "searching" than "researching." For example, for a typical high school senior, "researching" may involve reading the first three results from a Google search. As a result, some young people leave high school with a flawed understanding of the concept of research that may not be corrected until their third or fourth year of college. To make matters worse, those of us in academia have been known to throw around the term *research* generically, without a thorough explanation for students. Consider assignments that require students to do "scholarly research." We tend to worry over whether students comprehend the term *scholarly*, but perhaps *research* needs just as much attention. This lesson tackles this common oversight at a basic level by having students analyze different meanings of the term *research*.

LEARNING OUTCOME

The students will compare words that are often used synonymously with *research* in order to recognize that the term can have various meanings, depending on the situation.

PREPARATION

Pull entries for *research* from two or three dictionaries. Look for sources that give at least two definitions of *research;* one definition should relate to "the act of conducting a search," while the other should refer to or imply some sort of scholarly or studious *inquiry*. Note that the definitions in this lesson use *research* as a noun (and not as a verb). This choice is just a preference, because spending time on differences in parts of speech may complicate the learning outcome. Each pair of students will need a copy of the "Research Scenarios" worksheet (worksheet 3.1).

INSTRUCTION

◉ ACTIVITY ONE: COMPARE "SEARCH" AND "INQUIRY"

Class discussion, 10 to 15 minutes

On a screen or whiteboard, display the definitions of the term *research* that you gathered prior to the session. Point out that each dictionary provides a definition of "research" that uses both *search* and *inquiry* as descriptors. For example: *Merriam-Webster* defines *research* as "a careful or diligent *search*" and "studious *inquiry* or examination."[4] The *Oxford English Dictionary* defines *research* as "the act of *searching* carefully for or pursuing a specified thing or person," and "systematic investigation or *inquiry* aimed at contributing to knowledge of a theory, topic, etc., by careful consideration, observation, or study of a subject."[5]

To help shed light on the differences between the two concepts of *search* and *inquiry*, ask students to consider the definitions of "research" as a whole; for example, the choice of terms surrounding *inquiry* should imply some sort of scholarly research. Also, students may pick up on the fact that while the definitions that contain the term *search* tend to indicate a one-time event, the definitions related to *inquiry* denote a process that occurs over a period of time. For another approach, solicit examples from the students of times when they may have conducted a "careful search" and "studious or scholarly inquiry," or other descriptions found in the definitions you chose for the activity. They will likely describe *inquiry* as a more advanced or scholarly form of *search*.

◉ ACTIVITY TWO: RESEARCH SCENARIOS

Group work, class discussion, 15 to 20 minutes

Now that students have compared and contrasted the concepts of *search* and *inquiry*, they will apply their understanding of these words to real-life situations. Organize the students into pairs and ask each pair to complete the "Research Scenarios" worksheet (worksheet 3.1). The design of the questions challenges students to consider the meaning of all of the words in the scenarios. For instance, in the scenario "gathering facts in order to write a speech for class," the word "facts" *should* indicate a search for discrete information, rather than a scholarly inquiry. However, you should allow flexibility for various interpretations of the scenario based on reasonable justifications. If the worksheet seems too much of a challenge for a particular group of students, create scenarios with less ambiguity.

ASSESSMENT

Choose two or three pairs to explain which definitions they matched with each scenario in the worksheet and why. Students should recognize the complexity of the term *research*, and that it can vary based on a particular question or problem.

TERMINOLOGY

WORKSHEET 3.1

RESEARCH SCENARIOS

According to the *Merriam-Webster* dictionary, research can be defined as either:

1. "a careful or diligent search"
2. "studious inquiry or examination"

In each scenario below, you're in need of information. Decide which definition of *research* from the choices above best fits each scenario. Justify your response in writing. If you believe both definitions apply to a scenario, explain why.

a. Gathering facts in order to write a speech for class

b. Choosing a car to buy based on price and customer reviews

c. Measuring the potential market for your new business idea

d. Writing an argumentative paper for class that requires the use of information sources

NOTES

1. *Merriam-Webster Dictionary*, s.v. "Scholarly," www.merriam-webster.com/dictionary/scholarly.
2. *Oxford English Dictionary*, s.v. "Scholarly."
3. Google English Dictionary by Oxford Languages, s.v. "Scholarly."
4. *Merriam-Webster Dictionary*, s.v. "Research," www.merriam-webster.com/dictionary/research.
5. *Oxford English Dictionary*, s.v. "Research."

CHAPTER 4

METHODS OF INQUIRY

Some undergraduates may be fortunate enough to take courses on discipline-specific research methods. For those not in this group, the lessons in this chapter offer a general primer for students on research methods, with a focus on expanding their knowledge of the scientific method and recognizing basic differences between quantitative and qualitative research. This chapter does not involve instruction in statistics or the philosophy of science, topics that usually require a unique skill set to teach. Several Conversation Starters offer additional topics of discussion, however, if you have the expertise to take them on.

LESSON 17

SCIENTIFIC METHOD: ONE SIZE FITS ALL?

SUMMARY

Students identify the different elements that make up what they know to be the scientific method. They then analyze research scenarios within different disciplines to identify elements of the scientific method within each one.

SKILL LEVEL

Intermediate

CONTEXT

You may find that most undergraduates have learned in high school about some variant of what society colloquially refers to as the "scientific method." First-year students likely will describe this method as a set of steps that scientists use to conduct research. These steps might encompass asking questions, conducting experiments, analyzing data, and reaching conclusions. We know this to be a simplified explanation of scientific research, however. The term *scientific method* itself contributes to a narrow view of research and tends to imply a quantitative and objective approach. It can also be interpreted to exclude the social sciences and humanities. Without veering too far off-track into the fascinating field of the philosophy of science, a cursory survey of the literature reveals criticism of the notion of *the* scientific method. Instead, scholars choose *a* scientific method, one chosen based on the purpose and design of the research project at hand. For instance, the inductive method, the hypothetico-deductive method, the Bayesian method, and "inference to the best explanation" all function as types of scientific methods.[1] This lesson has a simple goal—to counteract the notion that one size of the scientific method fits all situations.

LEARNING OUTCOME

Students will develop a more sophisticated understanding of the concept of *scientific method* in order to accurately define and identify it.

PREPARATION

Sometimes the terms *hypothesis* and *theory* are used interchangeably. Although not the focus of this activity, be prepared to offer a brief description of the differences between these two terms if both of them come up in class discussion. Prepare a "Does One Size Fit All?" worksheet (worksheet 4.1) for each pair of students and supply each student with a note card. In its current form, this lesson requires internet access.

Here are some additional ideas to consider as you prepare:

- As a warm-up exercise, provide examples of various flowcharts and diagrams of the scientific method and let students vote on which one they believe to be the most accurate.
- Rather than students searching for flowcharts and diagrams of the scientific method in Activity One, have them sketch these out for themselves.

INSTRUCTION

ACTIVITY ONE: VISUALIZING THE SCIENTIFIC METHOD

Class discussion, group work 15 to 20 minutes

Ask each student to write anonymously on a note card any one step of the scientific method as they understand it. The use of the term *step* is intentional here, as this may be how most students envision the scientific method—as a set of steps. Students should be allowed to privately indicate on the card if they have no familiarity with the scientific method. Take up the note cards and solicit a volunteer. Call out the steps that the students wrote on the note cards as the volunteer transcribes them to a whiteboard. Guide the class to group similar descriptions of the same concepts together and bring attention to the major elements. Fill in the gaps as needed. The steps will likely include:

- Asking questions
- Developing hypotheses
- Testing hypotheses through experiments
- Analyzing the data or results of the experiments
- Accepting or rejecting the hypotheses

Explain to the students that an online search for images of "the scientific method" will reveal an endless number of diagrams and flowcharts that claim to represent the scientific method. Have the students work with a partner to search online for what they judge to be the most accurate visual representation of the scientific method. Allow volunteers to share some of their choices with the class. The majority of samples that students locate will no doubt illustrate the scientific method as a step-by-step linear process. Examples also exist, however, that suggest a more realistic, iterative approach. Call the students' attention to this significant discrepancy in conceptions of scientific research. Suggest to them that research and the scientific method function iteratively, and suggest one reason why a one-size-fits-all, step-by-step model of the scientific method does not work for all research.

ACTIVITY TWO: METHODS IN THE VARIOUS DISCIPLINES

Class discussion, group work 20 to 25 minutes

Begin with the statement and question: "We know that scientists use some sort of method to conduct research. What about social scientists or those who research in the humanities, such as historians?" This could prove a difficult question for undergraduates to answer, and how you explain this idea can vary. Group the students into pairs and have them consider the question further by completing the "Does One Size Fit All?" worksheet (worksheet 4.1). A review of the worksheet with the students should conclude with an understanding that both the type of research as well as discipline-specific factors can affect the method employed by scholars for a particular research project. Furthermore, the students should recognize more complexity in the concept of the scientific method than they did at the beginning of this lesson.

ASSESSMENT PROMPT

"How would you define the term *scientific method* to someone not familiar with it, so they could clearly understand it?"

WORKSHEET 4.1

DOES ONE SIZE FIT ALL?

Work with your partner to answer the questions below. These questions are intended to be answered using the critical thinking skills in your brain rather than searching the internet. In other words, there's not a "right" or "wrong" answer.

1. From research they have conducted, a historian hypothesizes that Europeans landed in America 100 years earlier than most historians believe. Describe a strategy that they could use to prove or disprove this hypothesis.

2. A sociologist hypothesizes that social media has altered how people interact with their neighbors. How might they conduct this research?

3. A chemist hypothesizes that mixing baking soda with milk is effective against tooth cavities. What sort of research could be conducted to test this hypothesis?

4. What are the similarities among the methods used above to conduct research? What are the differences?

LESSON 18

RESEARCH DESIGN

SUMMARY

The students brainstorm decisions that need to be made when designing something familiar to them. They apply that same procedure to the task of designing a research study.

SKILL LEVEL

Intermediate to Advanced

CONTEXT

Although we often conflate the two terms when teaching and conversing about research, John Creswell distinguishes between the concepts of *research design* and *research methods*. According to him, researchers can choose between three approaches to research design: quantitative, qualitative, and mixed approaches. *Research methods*, on the other hand, refers to the specific data-collection strategies used within the chosen design, such as statistics-gathering used in a quantitative study, and open-ended interviews used in a qualitative study.[2] Innumerable factors can influence the design a researcher chooses for a specific study. The students will explore some of the choices that need to be made before beginning a research study. This lesson provides more specific instruction on the differences between quantitative and qualitative research.

LEARNING OUTCOME

Students will learn about the decisions that should be made before conducting research in order to understand the importance of the research design process.

PREPARATION

In preparation for Activity Two, have the students brainstorm questions that scholars might address during the research design process. Examples include:

- What will you be studying? Humans, plants, outer space? What differences might you expect in research design if studying a living object compared to an inanimate object?

- What sort of data will you collect? How will you collect it? How much data do you need to collect?
- Will you use lab instruments? What other sorts of supplies do you require?
- Where will the research take place? In a lab, outside, or in an educational environment?
- How long will the research need to continue? One day, one week, one year, longer?

Each group of three or four students will need a copy of the "Designing a House" worksheet (worksheet 4.2) and a copy of the "Designing Research" worksheet (worksheet 4.3).

Here are some additional ideas as you prepare:

- Make the worksheet in Activity One a competition between the groups to brainstorm the most relevant questions.
- If the example of designing a house does not seem relatable to a particular group of students, choose something else. You could survey the class before the activity for ideas.
- If the worksheet in Activity Two seems too challenging, work through it with the class as a whole rather than using it as a small-group activity.

INSTRUCTION

ACTIVITY ONE: DESIGN A HOUSE

Class discussion, group work, 20 to 25 minutes

Let the students know that they will be learning about research design in this lesson, but as a warm-up exercise they will start off thinking about a different type of design. Divide the students into groups of three or four and hand each group a copy of the "Designing a House" worksheet (worksheet 4.2). Once completed, give each group the opportunity to share what they have prioritized as the most important questions. Explain to the class that they can apply this same concept to the idea of designing a research project or study. Continue with:

"Before you begin an experiment, or a survey, or whatever type of research you plan to conduct, you must come up with the research design. For instance, will you be researching humans or dogs? Your answer to this could mean a difference in how you carry out the research."

ACTIVITY TWO: DESIGN RESEARCH

Class discussion, group activity 20 to 25 minutes

Begin the second activity by surveying students on the questions they should ask when designing research. Refer to the questions you brainstormed prior to the session. After a brief discussion of these, the students return to their groups and complete the "Designing Research" worksheet (worksheet 4.3). Similar to the process in the first activity, give each group an opportunity to share what they consider as either the most critical questions to answer or the most important decisions to make for each of the research scenarios.

ASSESSMENT PROMPTS

- "Why is it important to design a research project before you attempt to conduct it?"
- "What are some questions that you should consider when designing a research project?"

WORKSHEET 4.2

DESIGNING A HOUSE

Imagine that you're a team of architects who have been hired to build a home for a family of four. The family consists of one adult and three children under the age of ten. You will need to brainstorm some questions to ask your clients about the design of the house. For example, how many bedrooms do they need? Take into account the size of the family, the age of the children, the family's dinner routine, etc.

Think of as many questions to ask as you can. Don't forget about the exterior of the home as well.

What are the three most important questions that you listed above?

WORKSHEET 4.3

DESIGNING RESEARCH

Your consulting firm works with scholars by helping them create effective research designs for their research studies. You currently have three clients. Brainstorm some questions related to research design that should be answered before each of the research projects described below can begin.

CLIENT 1:

Does studying a candidate's political platform influence whether someone changes their mind on who they plan to vote for?

CLIENT 2:

Do the chemicals in certain brands of pool chlorine cause birth defects?

CLIENT 3:

What determines the strength of a hurricane?

Did you list some of the same questions for each research question? If so, circle the ones that are related. Did you need to ask unique questions based on the research topic? If so, underline those.

LESSON 19

THE TWO Qs OF RESEARCH

SUMMARY

In this lesson, the students learn the meaning of *quantitative* and *qualitative* research and some characteristics of each of these types of research. They review examples of peer-reviewed articles that use quantitative and qualitative research and identify within those articles the characteristics they learned about in the first activity.

SKILL LEVEL

Advanced

CONTEXT

Quantitative and qualitative research design denote two major approaches to research. *Quantitative research* involves the collection and analysis of numerical and statistical data. Commonly used methods in this type of research include experiments of all kinds, observations recorded as numbers, and surveys that used closed questions (since these yield numerical data). Quantitative research is used to test and confirm (or reject) theories and hypotheses. *Qualitative research*, by contrast, involves the collection and analysis of non-numerical data—usually in the form of words and language. This research approach is often used to acquire in-depth insight into topics that are not well understood. The most commonly used methods in this type of research are interviews, surveys that use open-ended questions, and observations recorded in words (rather than numbers). More broadly, quantitative research can be characterized as objective because it deals with measurable quantities (numbers), while qualitative research can be characterized as subjective because it deals with phenomena (as expressed in words) which can be observed and interpreted but not measured.

Undergraduates who come to college with some training in the scientific method will probably be familiar with a quantitative approach to research, one that involves the collection of numerical data and the testing of hypotheses in a lab. By taking up this topic with undergraduates, you still risk leaving them with one main takeaway—quantitative research involves numbers, while qualitative research involves words. John Creswell, an author of numerous books about research design and methods, offers additional distinctions that go beyond the simplistic view of "numbers versus words." Some of these distinctions prove easy to spot; for instance, qualitative studies tend to use smaller samples than quantitative studies, and the objective-subjective distinction between the two approaches can also be quite apparent.[3] This lesson focuses on the more obvious differences between the two approaches, though.

LEARNING OUTCOME

Students will learn the different characteristics of quantitative and qualitative research in order to recognize the reasons why each could be chosen as an approach to research design.

PREPARATION

Choose an example of both a published quantitative and a published qualitative study for the second activity. You can establish the difficulty of the activity by selecting articles that clearly have the different characteristics discussed in Activity One, or by choosing articles that are less easily distinguishable in this regard. To help establish a pattern for students to see, choose two sets of articles each (four total) to distribute among the pairs of students. While there are always exceptions, table 4.1 offers suggestions on the characteristics to consider as markers of identification for each type of research approach.

Each pair of students will need a copy of the "QUAN or QUAL" worksheet (worksheet 4.4).

Here are some additional ideas to consider as you plan:

- Include mixed methods as a third research approach.
- If the "QUAN or QUAL" worksheet seems too advanced, work through it with the class as a whole.

INSTRUCTION

ACTIVITY ONE: DEFINING "QUANTITATIVE" AND "QUALITATIVE"

Class discussion, group work, 10 to 15 minutes

Review with the students the meanings of *quantitative* and *qualitative*. Questions to help introduce this topic include:

- When you hear the word *quantitative*, what comes to mind?
- What are the differences between the meanings of *quantitative* and *qualitative*?
- Explain to the class that scholarly research consists of three main approaches to research: quantitative, qualitative, and a mixture of the two.
- If we consider quantitative to be about collecting and analyzing numbers and data, what might we collect and analyze when conducting qualitative research?

	Quantitative	**Qualitative**
Disciplines	Natural and physical sciences	Social sciences
Location	In a research lab or other controlled environment	Within the environment of those being studied
Sample size	Probably large	Tends to be small
Data collection examples	Lab experiments	Open-ended interviews and observations
How data is presented	Charts and graphs	Textual explanations

TABLE 4.1 Characteristics of Quantitative and Qualitative Research Types

ACTIVITY TWO: IDENTIFYING QUAN AND QUAL RESEARCH

Group work, class discussion, 15 to 20 minutes

As the students organize into pairs, provide each pair with either copies or links to their assigned set of scholarly articles and a copy of the "QUAN or QUAL" worksheet (worksheet 4.4). Time the students so that they spend at least two minutes reviewing each article before answering the questions on the worksheet. Then lead the students in a discussion of their responses to the worksheet.

ASSESSMENT PROMPT

"Besides the obvious differences in the use of numbers and words, name another characteristic that can be used to differentiate quantitative from qualitative research."

WORKSHEET 4.4

QUAN OR QUAL

Take turns reviewing the articles. For the purpose of this activity, label one as Article 1 and the other as Article 2. Make note of which is which in the first two blanks. Complete the worksheet and be prepared to justify your responses to your classmates.

Article 1 _____

Article 2 _____

What discipline is being studied?

Article 1 _____

Article 2 _____

How is the data being collected?

Article 1 _____

Article 2 _____

How large is the sample?

Article 1 _____

Article 2 _____

What sorts of data are being collected?

Article 1 _____

Article 2 _____

How are the results presented?

Article 1 _____

Article 2 _____

One of the articles you're working with is a quantitative study and the other is a qualitative study. Based on the characteristics of each, which article is which?

CONVERSATION STARTERS

MIXED METHODS RESEARCH

As the third main approach to research design, mixed-methods research brings together aspects of the other two key approaches, quantitative and qualitative. This could be of particular relevance to undergraduates with interests in the social sciences and in interdisciplinary research. An advanced topic, these activities and discussions should be done in concert with lessons on quantitative and qualitative methods.

ACTIVITY IDEAS

- The students survey examples of mixed-methods research articles in order to identify their quantitative and qualitative aspects. Challenge the students to explain why the researchers chose mixed methods as the best approach for the research study.
- Assign the students a field of study and have them brainstorm research topics within that field which could be studied using a mixed-methods approach.

DISCUSSION QUESTIONS

- How would you define mixed methods research?
- What fields of study use mixed methods?
- Can mixed methods be used in the sciences? What about in the humanities?
- How does a mixed-methods approach add value to scholarly research?
- Is mixed-methods research worth it? In other words, do you think mixed methods complicates research? Explain why or why not.
- Can you think of a research topic that would benefit from the use of a mixed-methods approach?
- Some may think of mixed methods as being "the best of both worlds." Do you think this is true? Are there any downsides to a mixed-methods approach?
- What are the origins of mixed-methods research? Why is there a need for mixed methods in research?
- Explanatory design and exploratory design are two types of mixed-methods design.[4] How are these two different? Why might a researcher choose one over the other?

ARCHIVAL RESEARCH

In a general course on research methods, there may be a tendency to focus on traditional scientific research. However, archival research—most often associated with historical research—is alive and well. In fact, the growth in digital humanities research has opened the door to new and innovative uses of special collections and archival materials. You can challenge the students to align archival research with areas of research other than history.

ACTIVITY IDEAS

- Students of all majors tour the university archives. They consider ways that archival materials could be used in disciplines other than history.
- Assign undergraduates a digital collection that is available in your (or another) university archives. The students brainstorm research projects that could be conducted using the digitized materials.

DISCUSSION QUESTIONS

- What are archives?
- Are archives and special collections the same thing?
- What sort of degree or training is needed to be an archivist?
- What sorts of materials can be found in archival collections? Do you think this could change in the future?
- How would you define a primary source in the context of archival research? Is this different than how they define primary sources in your major?
- Is there value in archival research? Who or what benefits from archival research?
- What are some types of primary sources that a historian might use? What about a physicist?
- Would there be any reason for a chemist or other scholar in the sciences to use an archival collection to conduct research?
- Can you find archival collections online? If so, what sorts of institutions would make these available online?
- Can you think of examples of archives that you or your family members might maintain?
- Have you conducted archival research? If so, what aspect did you find most challenging?
- Does your university have an archive that can be visited? If so, where is it located?
- Why must items in an archival collection not be checked out or leave their physical location?
- How are archival research and digital humanities related?

REPRODUCIBILITY AND IRREPRODUCIBILITY

Reproducibility is the ability to re-create an experiment or research using the same method of another study and get similar results. This is how researchers verify others' results. Irreproducibility has an opposite meaning: research that is irreproducible cannot be reproduced or re-created with similar results. This type of research has proven to be an area of concern within the scholarly research ecosystem. Although this topic may at first seem too advanced for undergraduates, if we expect students to read and evaluate scholarly research, we should consider teaching them ways to recognize flaws in research methods.

ACTIVITY IDEAS

- Ask the students to locate and read commentary online about the issues surrounding the irreproducibility of research. They compare notes on what they learned in the readings.
- Provide a few irreproducible research studies for students to review. Challenge them to describe the flaws in the research.

DISCUSSION QUESTIONS

- What do *reproducibility* and *irreproducibility* mean?
- What are examples of things you do in your daily life that are either reproducible or irreproducible?
- What do these terms mean in relation to scholarly research?
- How does the reproducibility of results contribute to or detract from the validity and reliability of a research study?
- Why would a researcher want to test the reproducibility of an experiment or research study?
- What are some factors that could lessen the reproducibility of an experiment?
- Do you think it would be easier to reproduce the data from a quantitative study or from a qualitative study?
- How can you determine if a research study is reproducible?
- Why is reproducibility important to scholarly research?
- How might the irreproducibility of a research study affect the authority of the scholar who conducted the research?

DATA MANAGEMENT

Data management as a concept comprises complex issues and ideas with such importance that it has resulted in the rise of a specialty in academic librarianship. Although concern about data management in the context of scholarly research may not manifest for undergraduates, recognizing the significance of managing any set of self-created data is an information literacy philosophy that all students would benefit from knowing. Future graduate students might also appreciate such a discussion. The broad questions presented below could be focused to meet a particular instruction situation with the assistance of a colleague who has experience in teaching data management skills.

ACTIVITY IDEAS

- The students review selected scholarly articles and identify the data within the studies. They brainstorm ways that other scholars could potentially use the data.
- Assign the students an article to read about the importance of data management in research, written with limited professional jargon. Discuss with the students their thoughts on the topic.
- Invite a data management librarian to speak with students about their role and the importance of data management.

DISCUSSION QUESTIONS

- How do you define data?
- What types of information do you consider to be data? Do you think text can be considered data?
- What kinds of data have you collected in your day-to-day life? Have you organized the data? If so, why? Why have you saved this data?
- What does it mean to "manage" data? How do you manage data?
- What role does data play in scholarly research?
- What types of data might you collect if doing research in geology? What about sociology?
- Have you heard the phrase *research data management* used in relation to scholarly research? Do you know what the phrase means?
- Do scholars only share their research data in peer-reviewed articles? Are there other places where they can share their data?
- Is it necessary to retain research data after the results have been published?
- How could effectively managing the data used in a study support the reproducibility of the study?
- What could happen if the data gathered and used in a published research study is lost?
- How could a researcher make their data findable for others interested in their research?
- Are there places online where scholars can store their data? Can the university store it for them?
- Does your university have a plan for managing research data?

- Does your university have a librarian or other person available to help with the management of research data?

SCHOLARLY LITERATURE AND LITERATURE REVIEWS

If you use the term *literature* in a class of undergraduates for the first time, you can almost see their minds drifting to memories of reading *Beowulf* or the *Odyssey*. In other words, students need more explanation of what this word means in the context of scholarly research, especially if faculty require them to engage with scholarly literature. In this context, the word *literature* denotes the research or scholarship in a given field, and a *literature review* is a survey or discussion of the scholarly sources on a specific topic. However, the characteristics of literature reviews, such as purposes and types, tend to get less attention than other aspects of the research process in the undergraduate classroom. You should encourage faculty members to spend more time on this in class.

ACTIVITY IDEAS

- Because literature reviews vary so widely in their purpose, their placement within an article, and their coverage, undergraduates may have difficulty finding the literature review section within a scholarly article. Share with students a selection of scholarly articles with literature reviews that differ based on these characteristics. Instruct the students to identify the literature review in each article and its distinctive characteristics.
- Have students study literature reviews from different disciplines in order to identify unique characteristics in the structure or content of the reviews based on discipline.
- Scholarly articles can refer to the literature throughout an article, and therefore may not have a designated literature review section. Be sure to share examples with students in which this is the case.

DISCUSSION QUESTIONS

- What is "literature" in the context of scholarly research?
- What is the purpose of a literature review?
- What role does literature play in the scholarly conversation?
- Can scholarly literature be in a form other than text?
- What might it mean if a research study does not include a literature review?
- Is there a specific number of sources that should be included in a literature review?
- How are literature reviews for quantitative research written differently than those written for qualitative studies? What are the reasons for these differences?

- What is considered "literature" in the scholarly research ecosystem? Peer-reviewed articles? What about technical reports and conference proceedings?
- Where can you access scholarly literature? Can you find it in multiple places?
- What is the process by which scholarly literature is created?

CITATIONS

Students usually learn about citations in high school, but do they truly understand the purpose of citing sources, or why one professor might require MLA format while another prefers that they use the APA format? The answer to these questions is likely "no." Undergraduates would benefit from a discussion of *why* they must cite sources, in addition to the traditional how-to training. Furthermore, while students often learn about citations through the lens of avoiding plagiarism, a fresh perspective on how citations assist other scholars doing similar research could provide the students with a deeper appreciation of the importance of citing sources.

ACTIVITY IDEAS

- Choose two citation formats that your group of undergraduates have used or will be required to use in a particular class. Have them identify differences between the examples of citations that you provide. Challenge the students to brainstorm the reasons for those differences.
- Using a reliable website, ask students to explore the additional aspects of format style that extend beyond the citation, such as formatting, headings, and tables and figures.

DISCUSSION QUESTIONS

- Why must you cite your sources?
- How would you define the phrase *citation style*?
- Which citation styles have you used before? If you have used more than one style, do you find one easier to work with than the others? Why is this?
- Do citation styles differ from one discipline to another? And if so, why do you think this is the case?
- Why must all citations within in a paper be written in the same format?
- What are in-text citations? Why must you use them?
- Why do some in-text citations use authors' last names, and others use numbers?
- Is it acceptable to use an online citation-creation tool?
- Do you use a citation manager? If not, are you familiar with the purpose of such a tool?

- If you fail to cite a source, could you be accused of plagiarism?
- What does it mean to paraphrase a source? Is paraphrasing the same as summarizing? Explain.

NOTES

1. Brian D. Haig, "Scientific Method," in *Sage Reference Encyclopedia of Research Design*, ed. Neil J. Salkind (Thousand Oaks, CA: SAGE, 2010), 1326–29.
2. John W. Creswell and J. David Creswell, *Research Design: Qualitative, Quantitative, and Mixed Methods Approaches*, 5th ed. (Los Angeles: SAGE, 2018).
3. Creswell and Creswell, *Research Design*.
4. Creswell and Creswell, *Research Design*, 218.

CHAPTER 5

DISCIPLINES

Research method practices vary from discipline to discipline, as often does the purpose of the research. Undergraduates have few opportunities to explore these differences and why they matter. This chapter offers students a flavor of the types of research that occur in various areas of the liberal arts, with special attention paid to the purpose of non-science-related research and its benefits to society.

LESSON 20

START WITH THE LIBERAL ARTS

SUMMARY

Students will learn about the organizational structure of the liberal arts and the range of scholarly research that the liberal arts encompass.

SKILL LEVEL

Intermediate to Advanced

CONTEXT

Disciplines within the humanities, social sciences, and the natural sciences come together to make up what we call the liberal arts. Most colleges and universities require undergraduates to take a certain number of courses in each of these three areas; whether or not undergraduates use the term *liberal arts* to describe this collective can depend on socioeconomic factors. For instance, undergraduates who take college-prep courses in high school, or have family members who graduated from college, may enter their first year with prior exposure to the concept of the liberal arts. Others, however, such as some first-generation students, may have no context for the concept. Moreover, when you consider undergraduates beyond their first year of college, you can safely assume that most of them know little about research outside of their own area of study. Science students may not even realize that those in the humanities conduct research! If the undergraduates that you work with plan to continue into graduate school, they need an awareness of the big picture, which includes fields outside of their worldview that could offer opportunities for interdisciplinary research. This lesson includes a brief introduction to the liberal arts, with the main focus being the research approaches used within the three areas.

LEARNING OUTCOME

Students will explore the three traditional categories of the liberal arts in order to recognize basic similarities and differences in how the disciplines across the three categories conduct research.

PREPARATION

Create a survey of at least five questions using an audience-response tool that asks students to choose which "category"—humanities, social sciences, or natural sciences—a particular discipline falls into. Low-tech options such as students indicating their choices using note cards or raised hands would also work just fine. Choose a variety of disciplines that most students would be familiar with such as English, psychology, biology, social work, and history. Each group of three or four students will need a "Humanists, Social Scientists, or Natural Scientists" worksheet (see worksheets 5.1, 5.2, and 5.3), and you should prepare a slide to display the following questions:

- What do you study? People, places, the environment, or a combination?
- What are some words used to describe the type of research that you do? For example, *quantitative, statistical, objective, qualitative, descriptive, subjective*. List as many of these words as you can.
- How could research in this field benefit society?

Lastly, each student will need a note card or piece of paper.

Here are some additional ideas as you prepare:

- Assign each student a specific database to use for the worksheet in Activity Two or allow them to use Google Scholar.
- If it better meets the needs of your students, you can transform this lesson into one that focuses on fields that grant professional degrees, such as nursing, education, and engineering.
- Compare and contrast how a variety of universities and colleges organize the liberal arts disciplines by college or school.
- Explore courses that the university requires undergraduates to complete (e.g., two social sciences, two natural sciences, etc.) and discuss with the students their thoughts about the requirements.

INSTRUCTION

ACTIVITY ONE: LIBERAL ARTS CATEGORIES

Individual work, class discussion, 10 to 15 minutes

Ask students a few general questions to gauge their knowledge of the liberal arts, such as:

- What are the liberal arts?
- What are the three broad categories within the liberal arts?
- You probably have an idea of the sorts of disciplines categorized under the natural sciences. What about the humanities and social sciences?

Using the audience-response tool, lead the class through the pre-prepared questions in which they choose which category they believe a discipline belongs. Make time for a brief conversation about the response results of each question. Call on volunteers to answer the relevant discussion questions (and encourage them with small prizes or candy if needed):

- Could this discipline fall into more than one of the three categories? If so, why is that?
- If you chose a different answer than the one most of us agree is correct, are you willing to make an argument to convince your classmates that your choice is also correct?

ACTIVITY TWO: DISCIPLINES WITHIN THE CATEGORIES

Group work, class discussion, 25 to 30 minutes

Create groups of three or four students and hand each either a "Humanists," "Social Scientists," or "Natural Scientists" worksheet (worksheets 5.1, 5.2, and 5.3). Each of the three worksheet versions should be assigned to at least one group. Explain that the worksheet is a group activity, except for Question 2, which they will answer as individuals on the note cards. Display the slide you prepared to help guide the students' responses to that question. After completion, lead the students in a discussion about their answers to the worksheet.

ASSESSMENT

Use the completed worksheets to evaluate how well students identified similarities and differences in the types of research that occur within various disciplines of the liberal arts.

WORKSHEET 5.1

HUMANISTS

Scenario: Each person in your group is a humanist, yet you all conduct your research in different humanities disciplines.

1. Decide among yourselves which discipline that you each study and write your names in the blanks beside your choices.

   _____ is a Philosopher

   _____ is an Art Historian

   _____ is a Linguist

   _____ is a Theologist

2. Using a library database, each group member will explore research in your assigned discipline. Consider the questions on the screen and jot your individual answers down on your note card.

3. Come back together as a group and provide written answers to the questions below. Be prepared to share with the other groups.

   What are some common traits among these four disciplines? For instance, do they all study people? Do they all use statistics in their research?

   What are some differences? For instance, do you think research in some areas may have a greater impact on society than others? Explain.

   Do you think any of your disciplines would fit within another of the three categories, in addition to this one? Explain.

WORKSHEET 5.2

SOCIAL SCIENTISTS

Scenario: Each person in your group is a social scientist, yet you all conduct your research in different social science disciplines.

1. Decide among yourselves which discipline that you each study and write your names in the blanks beside your choices.

   _____ is an Anthropologist

   _____ is a Sociologist

   _____ is a Political Scientist

   _____ is a Historian

2. Using a library database, each group member will explore research in your assigned discipline. Consider the questions on the screen and jot your individual answers down on your note card.

3. Come back together as a group and provide written answers to the questions below. Be prepared to share with the other groups.

   What are some common traits among these four disciplines? For instance, do they all study people? Do they all use statistics in their research?

   What are some differences? For instance, do you think research in some areas may have a greater impact on society than others? Explain.

   Do you think any of your disciplines would fit within another of the three categories, in addition to this one? Explain.

WORKSHEET 5.3

NATURAL SCIENTISTS

Scenario: Each person in your group is a natural scientist, yet you all conduct your research in different scientific disciplines.

1. Decide among yourselves which discipline that you each study and write your names in the blanks beside your choices.

   _____ is a Biologist

   _____ is a Physicist

   _____ is a Geologist

   _____ is a Chemist

2. Using a library database, each group member will explore research in your assigned discipline. Consider the questions on the screen and jot your individual answers down on your note card.

3. Come back together as a group and provide written answers to the questions below. Be prepared to share with the other groups.

   What are some common traits among these four disciplines? For instance, do they all study people? Do they all use statistics in their research?

   What are some differences? For instance, do you think research in some areas may have a greater impact on society than others? Explain.

   Do you think any of your disciplines would fit within another of the three categories, in addition to this one? Explain.

95

LESSON 21

SCIENCE RESEARCH: THE FAMILIAR

SUMMARY

In this lesson, the students brainstorm a list of disciplines that they consider "sciences," consider an overarching definition of the term *science*, and compare and contrast research that occurs in different scientific disciplines.

SKILL LEVEL

Novice

CONTEXT

If you mention the word *research* to a group of undergraduates, you can expect their thoughts to land on some type of science. Why is this? *Science* serves as a broad and generic term—a catch-all of sorts—used by the general population, the media, K–12 teachers, and some college instructors as a descriptor, and possibly a synonym, for research. Generalizations like this should obviously be made with care, because exceptions will always exist. Overall, however, undergraduates, particularly first- and second-year students, equate scholarly research with science. Consider, for example, some of the research that college students have been exposed to in their lifetime: efforts to stop or reverse climate change, the discovery of a vaccine for a deadly disease, private companies creating their own rockets to go into space, and so on. Even with the growing popularity of interdisciplinary research, these research topics seem "sciency." This lesson will sharpen students' understanding of the idea of science by exploring the kinds of research that are carried out in specific fields of science. This approach can also serve as a foundation as students learn more about the less familiar social sciences.

LEARNING OUTCOME

Students will compare the characteristics of two scientific disciplines in order to recognize the differences in research methods and approaches among the various branches of science.

PREPARATION

Each student will require a copy of worksheet 5.4, the "Comparing Research in the Sciences" worksheet.

 CHAPTER 5

Here are some additional ideas as you prepare:

- Be prepared to be open-minded to students' responses in the first activity, since there is a degree of subjectivity in defining the subjects and areas of study within the sciences.
- If you feel a need to limit the responses in Activity One, ask the students to list only those scientific disciplines that are taught on your campus.
- The first activity could be a competition to see which pairs can list the most scientific disciplines.
- To reduce possible confusion, try to be consistent in how you will refer to the different sciences, whether it be *kinds*, *types*, *disciplines*, *fields*, *subjects*, or *areas*.

INSTRUCTION

ACTIVITY ONE: WHAT IS A SCIENCE?

Group work, class discussion, 15 to 20 minutes

Begin with an open question such as "How do you define science?" or "What comes to mind when someone mentions scientific research?" The students' answers may vary widely, leading to a possibly interesting and lively discussion. Transition to the first activity by arranging the students into pairs. The students will be given two minutes to list on a piece of paper as many areas of science as possible without the use of the internet. After the two minutes expire, solicit a whiteboard scribe. The pairs will take turns sharing one of the scientific disciplines that they listed as the scribe writes them on the board. This activity continues until there are no new scientific disciplines to add to the board. A brief discussion could include these questions:

- Do you disagree with any of the subjects listed on the board? Explain.
- What do these subjects have in common? Do they study similar things?
- Now that you can see this long list, would this change your definition of science?
- Can you fill in the blank in the sentence, "Science is the study of _____?

You can steer the discussion to research through additional questions:

- Can you think of similarities or differences in the type of research that might occur in these different areas?
- Do all of these areas use the scientific method?

ACTIVITY TWO: SCIENCE RESEARCH

Group work, class discussion, 15 to 20 minutes

Assign one of the scientific disciplines written on the board to each student. Consider assigning two sciences that have obvious differences in approaches, methods, or subjects of research, for example, geology and physics, to each pair of students. Each student receives a "Comparing Research in the Sciences" worksheet (worksheet 5.4). Review the instructions with the class. Be sure to tell the students when to swap sciences with their partners. Give the pairs time to compare their answers for both sciences, and then ask for volunteers to share their points of agreement and disagreement.

ASSESSMENT PROMPT

"What is one unique characteristic of research for each of the two areas of science that you reviewed?"

WORKSHEET 5.4

COMPARING RESEARCH IN THE SCIENCES

Write the scientific discipline that you were given in the blank below. Then, using the internet if needed, answer the questions below. When time is called, you and your partner will compare your responses.

Science _____

What is one main purpose of research in this area of science?

Where are some places that researchers in this science conduct their research? You may have more than one answer (for example, on a ship, in a lab, in the desert).

What are some kinds of equipment that researchers in this area of science need in order to conduct research?

How can research in this particular area of science benefit society?

LESSON 22

SOCIAL SCIENCE RESEARCH: THE LESS FAMILIAR

SUMMARY

In this lesson, the students define *social science* through class discussion, and then consider the purposes of social science disciplines by contemplating various social science research topics.

SKILL LEVEL

Novice to Intermediate

CONTEXT

You may find that first- and second-year undergraduates exhibit less familiarity with the social sciences than with the other areas of the liberal arts. Of course, high school curricula have traditionally emphasized the sciences and humanities, with less focus on the social sciences. Looking at this from a different perspective, students' penchant to associate research with the sciences could be traced back to their training on the scientific method in K–12. The scientific process is often presented as a linear one—you find a problem, develop a hypothesis, do an experiment to test the hypothesis, and determine whether you proved your hypothesis. The simplicity of this model fits well for research that high school students take part in, often experiments in science labs, but not so neatly with social science research. Therefore, the purpose and value of social science research may be unclear to some because of their unfamiliarity with these disciplines. Given the growing significance of interdisciplinary research, this lesson will bolster the understanding of all students, especially those who are interested in social science research.

LEARNING OUTCOME

Students will reflect on examples of research topics in the social sciences in order to appreciate the value of social science research.

PREPARATION

Create a slide deck with one branch of the social sciences displayed on each slide. You might consider sociology, political science, economics, anthropology, psychology, and history; these examples are intended to allow for flexibility, given that history, for example, can also be considered one of the humanities. Each student will need a copy in print or an online version of the "Value of the Social Sciences" worksheet (worksheet 5.5). Activity Two could be either an individual or group activity.

INSTRUCTION

ACTIVITY ONE: DEFINING SOCIAL SCIENCE

Class discussion, 15 to 20 minutes

Begin with one or two discussion questions. For example, "How is the study of social sciences different than the study of sciences? What about humanities?" If the idea of social sciences is new to this group of students, you will need to begin more basically, by asking, "What is a social science?" Flip through the pre-prepared slides, spending a few minutes on each social science, and letting students share what they know and understand about each one. Ask a volunteer to keep track of the main themes on a whiteboard or in writing. This list should include words such as *humans*, *cultures*, *systems*, *relationships*, *societies*, and *behavior*. Guide the class to create a definition of social science, using some or all of the main themes identified. For instance, "the study of societies and the relations among individuals within those societies" or, to keep it simple, "the study of human behavior and society."

ACTIVITY TWO: RESEARCH IN THE SOCIAL SCIENCES

Individual work, class discussion: 15 to 20 minutes

Now that the students have an agreed-upon understanding of the social sciences, turn the focus specifically to social science research. Each student will complete the "Value of the Social Sciences" worksheet (worksheet 5.5), which should result in a class discussion about the value of research in the social sciences.

ASSESSMENT PROMPTS

- "What are some purposes of research in the social sciences?"
- "What differences do you recognize between the purposes of social science research and the purposes of scientific research?"

WORKSHEET 5.5

VALUE OF THE SOCIAL SCIENCES

Read each research topic below and answer the corresponding questions to the best of your ability. Be ready to discuss your responses.

1. Research topic: What environmental factors determine how high school students perform on standardized tests?

    What social sciences might study this topic?

    How could this research benefit society?

2. Research topic: How do presidential elections affect the U.S. economy?

    What social sciences might study this topic?

    How could this research benefit society?

3. Research topic: What have been the most common reasons for armed conflict between sovereign nations over the last century?

   What social sciences might study this topic?

   How can this research benefit society?

4. Research topic: How do eating habits at home affect a child's success in school?

   What social sciences might study this topic?

   How can this research benefit society?

LESSON 23

DIGITAL HUMANITIES

SUMMARY

Students reflect on what they know about the humanities and explore various digital humanities projects to consider how this type of scholarly research can contribute to society.

SKILL LEVEL

Intermediate

CONTEXT

The humanities are academic disciplines that study human culture. The subjects of the humanities include languages and literature, religion, philosophy, and the arts. This lesson centers on helping undergraduates gain an appreciation for humanities research. Although many universities and colleges require students to take a certain number of humanities courses, the purpose of humanities research can be difficult for undergraduates to define. This rings especially true for students with majors in the sciences and social sciences. Furthermore, this lesson introduces students to the relatively new field of digital humanities, thus allowing them to explore the practical applications of humanities research. Please note: this lesson does not imply that humanities research which does not intersect with digital technologies results in scholarly contributions of lower quality or less importance; rather, the example of *digital humanities* is used in this lesson because it can quickly and effectively help undergraduates visualize the possibilities of the humanities. This lesson obviously touts the benefits of the humanities, but it could be altered to take a more critical or balanced approach. For example, students could compare the potential outcomes of humanities research with the more exacting measures and results used in scientific research; they could be asked to justify why or why not grant money should be earmarked for the humanities; or they could react to less-than-stellar examples of digital humanities projects.

LEARNING OUTCOME

Students will consider research in the humanities in order to appreciate what the humanities can offer to society.

PREPARATION

As you prepare for Activity One, create a list of terms or a definition that illustrates how the humanities impact society. Although a list like this can be subjective, your list might explain that through the humanities we learn about people, their histories, and their cultures. Knowing more about others—especially those different from us—can cultivate empathy and a better understanding of current equity and social justice issues. In another example, if you categorize history as one of the humanities, undergraduates will likely respond to the adage that "we learn from the past" or other variant statements about the pitfalls of repeating history. Prepare a slide with various humanities-related research topics. You could be less specific by listing disciplines such as "literature," but it may be more difficult for students to express how humanities research from such a broad perspective would benefit society. Example topics include:

- How religion influenced the art of the ancient Greeks.
- The role that ethics plays in labor disputes.
- The impact of politics on nineteenth-century poetry.

Digital humanities, the focus of Activity Two, is a complex subject. The activity should serve only as a brief introduction to this form of scholarly research. Be prepared to explain the purpose of digital humanities to students in a succinct manner. For instance:

- The digital humanities are humanities studies that systematically use digital or computing technologies.
- The use of digital technology allows researchers to analyze humanities data in new ways.
- Digital technology lets those of us in the general population gain a better understanding of humanities studies by interacting with them online.

Each group of three or four students will need a "Digital Humanities Project" worksheet (worksheet 5.6). Choose four or five digital humanities projects in different fields. Examples include the Music Encoding Initiative, Slave Voyages, Digital Thoreau, the Internet Philosophy Ontology Project, and the Perseus Project. The students will require internet access for both activities in this lesson.

INSTRUCTION

ACTIVITY ONE: INTRODUCTION TO THE HUMANITIES

Class discussion, group work, 15 to 20 minutes

Begin the session by holding a conversation with students about what they know about the humanities. Here are some discussion questions:

- Have you heard people refer to "the humanities?" If so, what does that phrase mean to you?

- Do you know if you have taken courses in the humanities? If so, what were they?
- Why does the university require you to take a certain number of courses in the humanities?

This last question would apply to those at institutions with general education or core curriculum course requirements. After laying this groundwork, continue asking students to describe what they know about the humanities. Example prompts include:

- What do scholars in the humanities teach and research?
- What do the humanities teach us? What is an example of a discipline in the humanities, and what can we learn from that discipline?
- Unlike science, research in the humanities most likely won't cure illnesses, and it may not help us solve current societal problems, as does research in the social sciences. So what is the value of the humanities to society?

Organize the students into pairs, display the pre-prepared slide, and assign each pair of students a research topic listed on the slide. Give the students a few minutes to discuss how research on their assigned topic could affect people, cultures, or society as a whole. Encourage volunteers to share their thoughts, and then lead the class as they develop an overarching definition for the humanities based on the class discussion.

ACTIVITY TWO: INTRODUCTION TO THE DIGITAL HUMANITIES

Class discussion, group work, 20 to 25 minutes

Explain briefly about the digital humanities as a field of research. Arrange the students into groups of three and assign each group one of the pre-selected digital humanities projects. Instruct them to complete the "Digital Humanities Project" worksheet as a group (worksheet 5.6). Because the projects tend to be visually appealing, allow the groups to share each project with their classmates, and guide the students as they discuss the merits of each project.

ASSESSMENT PROMPTS

- "Describe one way that research in the humanities can have a positive influence on society."
- "How can digital technologies enhance research in the humanities?"

WORKSHEET 5.6

DIGITAL HUMANITIES PROJECT

Name of project: _____

Who is responsible for this project? For instance, a university, a corporation, or a group of individuals?

What humanities disciplines are represented in this project?

How does this project help us better understand the topic that it presents?

Who might use this information? Do you see this being used in other humanities fields, or even the sciences and social sciences? Think creatively.

CONVERSATION STARTERS

INTERDISCIPLINARY RESEARCH

Of increasing significance within the scholarly research ecosystem, interdisciplinary research supports the notion of a "messy" research process, one that may require or benefit from collaborations between scholars in multiple fields using multiple methods. This can give undergraduates a richer interpretation of the research process. It can also give them more appreciation for fields within academia that may not have an obvious or immediate impact in terms of problem-solving or innovation via their research.

ACTIVITY IDEAS

- Provide the students with a list of interdisciplinary research topics and ask them to list all of the potential disciplines that might be part of each project.
- Have the students review published interdisciplinary research studies and parse out what each researcher contributed to the study. Have the students consider how the study would have proceeded without expertise in all of the disciplines included.

DISCUSSION QUESTIONS

- How would you define interdisciplinary research (IR)?
- What are some benefits of IR that are not possible with single-discipline research?
- Why is IR important to science? What about the social sciences and humanities?
- Brainstorm some examples of interdisciplinary research topics.
- How might IR promote more openness and trust in the world of scholarly research?
- Does the university take part in or promote IR? Where could you find this information?
- Are there financial benefits to IR? If so, who or what benefits?
- What might be some drawbacks to IR? Do you think the pros outweigh the cons?
- How is IR conducted? Is it quantitative? Can you use a mixed-methods approach?
- What would be some of the considerations regarding research methods when designing an interdisciplinary study?

CHAPTER 6

DISSEMINATION AND ACCESS

Although *dissemination* and *access* are discrete concepts, the interconnections between them with regard to scholarly research make them difficult to unravel from one another. For example, what are the roadblocks to access if a researcher chooses to publish (i.e., disseminate) their research in a subscription-based scholarly journal? Who do these roadblocks affect the most? These questions consider both dissemination and access issues. The lessons in this chapter will allow you to explore these types of critical questions with your students.

LESSON 24

THE JOB OF SCHOLARLY JOURNALS

SUMMARY

Students brainstorm the purposes of scholarly journals, and then consider how these journals support scholarly conversations and scholarly communication.

SKILL LEVEL

Novice to Intermediate

CONTEXT

Library instruction one-shot sessions that introduce students to scholarly articles—and as a consequence, scholarly journals—have traditionally focused on the peer-review process, whether the author has the proper credentials to publish within a particular field, and certain distinctive elements (abstracts, reference lists, etc.) that distinguish scholarly journals from magazines and newspapers. For those of us who have been in the profession for a few decades, you have probably told a class at one time or another that "scholarly journals don't have ads" or "scholarly journals are printed in mostly black and white." As print journals were replaced by electronic versions, however, many librarians began to move away from the reliance on physical characteristics, or format, as the nucleus of this instruction. Instead, they developed lessons and activities that require students to think more critically about the purposes of scholarly journals. The activities in this lesson present one such approach, by connecting scholarly journals to scholarly conversations and scholarly communication, defined here as the conduits and channels by which scholars communicate.

LEARNING OUTCOME

The students will consider how scholarly journals support scholarly conversations and scholarly communication in order to understand the function of these journals within the scholarly research ecosystem.

PREPARATION

For use in the first activity, create a free-form survey using an audience response tool with the question, "Based on what you already know, what is the purpose of a scholarly journal?" To encourage student participation, make sure the responses will display anonymously. In addition, make copies of the "Conversations and Communication" worksheet (worksheet 6.1) for each pair of students. Internet access will likely be needed to complete the worksheet.

INSTRUCTION

ACTIVITY ONE: SHARING RESEARCH WARM-UP

Individual work, class discussion, 10 to 15 minutes

Ask each student to respond using the audience-response tool to the question that you prepared before the session. After students have submitted their responses anonymously, display the results on the projector screen. Address all the relevant responses, although the answers will likely center around "sharing research." Explain to the students that they will explore this idea further in the next activity.

ACTIVITY TWO: SCHOLARLY CONVERSATIONS AND COMMUNICATION

Group work, class discussion, 15 to 20 minutes

Arrange the students into pairs and give each pair a copy of the "Conversations and Communication" worksheet (worksheet 6.1). After the students complete the worksheet, discuss their responses with them, emphasizing the themes that show how scholarly journals support scholarly conversations as a form of scholarly communication and why this is important.

ASSESSMENT PROMPT

"Explain the relationship between scholarly journals, scholarly communication, and the scholarly conversation."

WORKSHEET 6.1

CONVERSATIONS AND COMMUNICATION

We can agree that scholarly journals allow scholars to share their research with one another. Discuss the following questions with your partner and write down your responses on this worksheet.

What are ways that scholars communicate in addition to scholarly journals? List at least three.

What differentiates scholarly journals from other modes of scholarly communication?

You may hear your professors say that publishing research in a scholarly journal is a way to have conversations with other researchers. Explain how conversations occur through scholarly journals.

How might scholarly research be different if scholarly journals didn't exist?

LESSON 25

CHOOSING WHERE TO PUBLISH

SUMMARY

Students learn why scholars should compare the various attributes of scholarly journals when choosing where to submit their research for possible publication. They weigh these options for themselves in a real-world scenario.

SKILL LEVEL

Advanced

CONTEXT

This lesson undertakes two goals. First, it illustrates to students how certain attributes of scholarly journals such as disciplinary focus, format of articles, and acceptance rate can help to distinguish or categorize journals. Second, some of these critical attributes discussed may be unfamiliar to students, providing an opportunity to briefly introduce concepts such as open access and authors' rights. The lesson will probably be most effective with undergraduates who understand the purposes of scholarly journals, and who possibly have searched scholarly journals while finding sources for their own research. In addition, the focus of this lesson may be most suitable for students planning to attend graduate school. However, even for undergraduates who have other intentions after graduation, the activities in this lesson can help them identify aspects of scholarly publishing they may still encounter in some way.

LEARNING OUTCOME

The students will learn about the attributes that distinguish scholarly journals from one another in order to appreciate how these differences can affect where scholars choose to submit their research for publication.

PREPARATION

Create a slide of each of the various characteristics of scholarly journals. These will serve as discussion prompts for the question "What should a scholar consider about scholarly journals when deciding to publish their research?" Suggested characteristics to include are:

- Type of content
- Subject focus
- Format of peer-reviewed articles
- Copyright policies
- Access policies of the publisher
- Journal ranking and acceptance rate

Be prepared with succinct descriptions of features that may be less familiar or new to students, such as journal ranking and authors' rights. Also, choose a journal website that addresses most of these features to use as an example in Activity One. The second activity requires a copy of the "Choosing a Scholarly Journal" worksheet (worksheet 6.2) for each student. In addition, choose two scholarly journals and a research article, all in the same field, to use as examples. Your choices of examples should be influenced by the level of complexity desired for this exercise. The greater the similarity of attributes between two journals, the more challenging the activity will be for students. Also, consider how the answers to the worksheet questions could affect the conversation; if one journal meets none of the criteria, and the other meets all of the criteria, this oversimplifies the process. The students will require internet access for both activities.

Additional ideas to consider as you prepare:

- This activity does not take into account all the individual motivations for choosing a journal, such as the factors someone working to achieve tenure might prioritize based on their departmental and university expectations. These nuances could be incorporated, however.
- For courses in specific disciplines, focus the activities on scholarly journals within that area (e.g., chemistry, biology, history, etc.).

INSTRUCTION

ACTIVITY ONE: WHAT TO CONSIDER

Class discussion, group work, 15 to 20 minutes

Establish a scenario with the class in which students must choose the most appropriate scholarly journal in which to publish their research. Engage in discussion with students as you go through each of the pre-prepared slides, providing explanations for concepts that are new to them. Show the class the website of a scholarly journal. Give them time to explore the site to find information in that journal about the attributes you just covered.

ACTIVITY TWO: CHOOSING A JOURNAL

Class discussion, group work, 25 to 30 minutes

Either on a slide or whiteboard, share the names of the two scholarly journals that you chose for this activity. Provide each pair of students with a copy of the scholarly article and a copy of the "Choosing a Scholarly Journal" worksheet (worksheet 6.2). Explain that though it has already been published, they should treat the scholarly article as the draft article referred to in the worksheet scenario (for greater authenticity, prior to class you could remove the name of the journal, the publication date, and other identifying markers on the article copies). Review the scenario with the class and give them ample time to complete the worksheet. Lead a class discussion afterwards, allowing students to share with each other their thoughts and opinions about choosing where to publish.

ASSESSMENT PROMPT

"Explain why authors' rights should be a factor to consider when choosing a scholarly journal in which to submit research for potential publication."

WORKSHEET 6.2

CHOOSING A SCHOLARLY JOURNAL

You both work as assistants for a new Biology research professor. The professor has chosen two scholarly journals as possible places to submit their first research article for publication. The professor has asked you to collaborate as a team to compare certain characteristics of both journals and report back in order to help them decide which to choose.

You will each examine one of the journals and then come together to discuss your findings and choose the journal that you believe best matches your professor's desired requirements. Explore the journal websites and other websites as needed in order to provide accurate information. Your professor is particularly interested in the journal's:

- subject content
- access policies
- copyright policies
- format of articles

Name of Journal: _____

1. Is the topic of your professor's article similar to topics published in the journal? Explain.

2. Is this an open access journal? Your professor would like as many people as possible to access their article.

3. Must your professor give up their copyrights to the article if they publish in this journal? Your professor would like to retain their copyrights.

Do the articles follow a similar format to your professor's article? For example, do most of the articles have a literature review, methods and discussion sections, etc.? Your professor feels that their article will have a better chance of acceptance if the format aligns with other articles in the journal.

LESSON 26

SUBSCRIPTIONS TO SCHOLARLY RESEARCH

SUMMARY

Students search for specific scholarly articles using the strategies of their choice. They learn that access to an article usually depends on whether the university library has paid a subscription fee for access to the journal in which that article was published. Students then explore journals' websites to learn more about the costs and policies of journal subscriptions.

SKILL LEVEL

Intermediate

CONTEXT

When discussing access to scholarly research with undergraduates, you could emphasize journal subscriptions, database subscriptions, or both. If not careful, you could also find yourself presenting complex access issues to students that librarians themselves grapple with every day. This lesson is designed to enlighten students about research using subscription-based scholarly journals, while keeping students out of the thick and unwieldy weeds of dissemination and access. The topic could be approached from various angles, however. Knowing that individuals or libraries must pay for access to most scholarly research dovetails with concepts from the *Framework for Information Literacy for Higher Education*. These concepts include "Information Creation as a Process," "Information Has Value," "Searching as Strategic Exploration"—in fact, you could make a case for this lesson's ties to most of the frames in the *Framework*.[1] An awareness of journal subscriptions and how they work in the context of scholarly research should foster in the students an appreciation for the convenience of open access and for the role of libraries in breaking through paywalls. This lesson necessitates that students have some familiarity with scholarly journals.

LEARNING OUTCOME

The students will gain an understanding of the subscription costs that libraries pay for access to scholarly research in order to recognize why they may not be able to access all scholarly articles online.

PREPARATION

Choose two citation examples—the first of an article that is available through your library via subscription, and the second for one that is not available. For the second activity, choose two or three scholarly journals published by different commercial publishers that require subscriptions. Also include an example of a journal published by an academic or professional organization. You should aim for journals that provide individual subscription information on their websites. Each group of students will need access to the "Journal Subscriptions" worksheet (worksheet 6.3). One last thought: to help with simplicity, this lesson does not differentiate between publishing companies and vendors of aggregated search products.

INSTRUCTION

ACTIVITY ONE: ACCESS VIA SUBSCRIPTIONS

Individual work, class discussion, 15 to 20 minutes

Display the slide deck with the example citations. Ask the students to work individually to locate the first article on the internet. Because this requires them to understand how to read citations, it may be helpful to review the parts of the citation with them, making sure they can distinguish the article's title from the journal title. Instruct the class to use whatever strategy they want to locate a copy of the article. Undergraduates will probably begin in one of four places—Google, Google Scholar, the search box on the home page of the university library, or a library database. Where they choose will likely depend on their college grade level and whether they have had some form of library or information literacy instruction. Be clear that they should find the full text of the article, not just the abstract. You have a few options on how to discuss their chosen search strategies:

- If students searched Google or Google Scholar and found the first article, explain that they were able to access the article because the library subscribes to the journal and because they searched for it while physically on campus. If visible on the website or article, point out the "access provided by your library" icon. Explain to the students that if they search off-campus, they should follow certain steps to authenticate so that the full-text links will be available to them.
- If students searched for the first article in a specific library database and did not locate the article, you should explain the difficulty in guessing which database to search when looking for a specific article, and the alternatives to that approach.
- For the second article, you could see a couple of scenarios: students locate the citation on Google or Google Scholar, but run into a paywall; or they search the library database's search box and find nothing. Use this as a chance to introduce the issue of subscription costs and why individual university libraries usually cannot purchase access to all scholarly journals. You could bolster

your explanation with a discussion of how the type of research taking place at a university, as well as the courses and subjects taught, influence the school's decisions about which subscriptions to purchase. For instance, if a university does not have a medical school, the library will not invest heavily in subscriptions to resources that would support a medical school.

ACTIVITY TWO: THE MONEY FACTOR

Class discussion, 20 to 25 minutes

This activity digs deeper into the practices of journal publishers. It is also a chance to introduce students to terms such as *paywall* and *open access*. Remember to keep the explanations simple, though, as in "open access journals have no subscription fees, but most journals are still published on a subscription-based model." Organize the students into groups of two or three and provide each group with access to the "Journal Subscriptions" worksheet (worksheet 6.3). Pull up the journal list that you prepared prior to the session and ask the groups to count off, assigning a journal to each of them based on their numbers. Then ask them to complete the worksheet based on the journal assigned to them. Here are a few points to consider for a post-worksheet discussion:

- Institutional subscription costs can be difficult, if not impossible, to find on a journal's website. Here you could explain how the cost of a journal (or a "bundle" of journals) can vary from university to university because publishers allow institutions to create tailored subscription packages, and publishers often give discounts for large subscriptions, thus determining the price on a case-by-case basis.
- Why is the cost of an individual journal subscription usually different than that cost of a subscription for the entire university?
- Why do publishers make authors pay to publish their work in an open access journal?

ASSESSMENT PROMPT

"If your friend could not access a scholarly article that they needed for their research, what possible explanations for this lack of access would you offer to them?"

WORKSHEET 6.3

JOURNAL SUBSCRIPTIONS

Work with your teammates to complete this worksheet. You will need to use the journal's website to answer the questions.

Assigned Journal: _____

What company or institution publishes this journal?

How many issues are published of this journal per year?

Can individuals purchase subscriptions to this journal? If so, what is the cost?

What can you find out about institutional subscriptions of this journal, such as for universities?

Does the publisher of the journal offer open access options? If so, do they require the author to pay a fee to publish?

LESSON 27

OPEN ACCESS

SUMMARY

The students brainstorm examples of services or companies that offer both free and subscription-based services or entertainment. You help students draw parallels between these familiar models and open-access scholarly publishing. The students then consider a scenario about which open-access scholarly journal they would choose to publish an article in.

SKILL LEVEL

Intermediate to Advanced

CONTEXT

Open-access scholarly publishing represents a significant advance in the scholarly publishing model—a model that has traditionally benefited the publishing companies, which reap large fees from subscriptions to the journals they publish. Libraries still have work to do, however, to wrest the research funded and produced by universities away from commercial publishers and from behind expensive paywalls. Open access gives us the chance to chip away at these unfortunate circumstances and avoid exorbitantly high subscription fees. To continue forward progress in this regard, students with plans to continue in academia and research *must* learn about open access options. To get the most out of this lesson, students should already be familiar with the concept of subscription journals and databases.

LEARNING OUTCOME

Students will understand the concept of open access in the context of scholarly research in order to recognize that scholars have opportunities to retain some or all control over their published scholarly work.

PREPARATION

For Activity Two, prepare enough "Open Access Policies" worksheets (worksheet 6.4) for each pair of students. Choose three journals (in the same field of study, if possible) that can be found on the Sherpa Romeo website, and add the titles of all three to a slide.[2] The difficulty of the activity can be altered by the types of journals you choose. For instance, the more similarity in the publishers' policies regarding open access among the journals, the more critical thinking will be required of the students. This lesson requires internet access.

INSTRUCTION

ACTIVITY ONE: WHAT'S THE CATCH?

Class discussion, 10 to 15 minutes

Have students brainstorm some entertainment companies that offer free versions of their products. Obvious examples include different formats of streaming media that display advertisements every few songs or minutes, and "free" versions of game apps that often come with fewer features than the for-purchase versions. Lead the students with a couple of questions:

- What are the benefits to companies to offer free versions of their products?
- If students fail to mention it, remind them that by offering these free services to everyone, companies can potentially increase the number of paid subscriptions.
- Are these truly "free" versions? Are there inconveniences to the free versions?
- Students should recognize the purpose of pop-up advertising and any other ways companies can recoup their costs by offering "free" versions of their products. Conclude with the notion that "free" versions usually have limited features in comparison to the subscription versions, and that comparable models of doing business in this way can be found in the world of scholarly publishing.

ACTIVITY TWO: OPEN ACCESS POLICIES

Class discussion, group work, 20 to 25 minutes

Remind the class that the university library pays subscription fees to access most scholarly journals. However, many publishers of scholarly journals offer an "open access" option. This means that if a scholar chooses to publish their work as open access, anyone with internet access can read their research, without a paid subscription or affiliation with a university library. Ask the students to list some of the benefits of open access publishing. If not reflected in their responses, explain that open access greatly expands the number of people who can access the research. This can benefit the journal, the author, and those doing similar research. Continue with: "Similar to what we discussed regarding the free versions of entertainment that you can find on the internet, most scholarly journals that allow scholars to publish open access have stipulations about how the research can be shared."

Introduce students to the Sherpa Romeo website. Do a few journal title searches on the site and show students the site's "Publisher Policies." The discussion should introduce students to the concepts of publishing embargos, author copyrights, repositories, and publishing fees. Note that the purpose of introducing these concepts is not for students to leave with a sophisticated understanding of them, but rather to recognize basic ways that these factors can make research more "open." Allow the students to partner with a neighbor, and then pass out the "Open Access Policies" worksheet (worksheet 6.4) to each pair of partners. Give the pairs a chance to share and justify their choices with the class. To encourage a lively discussion, challenge the entire class to agree on the best choice.

ASSESSMENT PROMPT

"In your opinion, which policy of open access journals should scholars consider the most crucial when choosing where to publish? Explain your answer."

WORKSHEET 6.4

OPEN ACCESS POLICIES

You and your research partner want to publish an open access article. Search the Sherpa Romeo website for each of the journals on the slide to determine the one that has the fewest limits on open access. Answers the questions below for each journal.

JOURNAL 1

Is there an embargo on articles published in the journal? If so, how long does it last?

Who holds the copyright to articles published in the journal?

Where can open-access copies of the articles be published?

Can you post copies of the submitted or accepted versions of the article online?

JOURNAL 2

Is there an embargo on articles published in the journal? If so, how long does it last?

Who holds the copyright to articles published in the journal?

Where can open-access copies of the articles be published?

Can you post copies of the submitted or accepted versions of the article online?

JOURNAL 3

Is there an embargo on articles published in the journal? If so, how long does it last?

Who holds the copyright to articles published in the journal?

Where can open-access copies of the articles be published?

Can you post copies of the submitted or accepted versions of the article online?

Which journal do you believe could be considered the most "open" in terms of open access? The choice may not be obvious—you will need to come to an agreement with your partner on the factors that you consider most important.

Which journal would you choose?

CONVERSATION STARTERS

SCHOLARLY JOURNAL RANKINGS

Although a more advanced topic, a conversation about journal rankings could dovetail with lessons on dissemination, scholarly conversations, faculty tenure decisions, issues of diversity and inclusion in scholarly publishing, and information has value, just to name a few.

ACTIVITY IDEAS

- The students explore Google Scholar's journal rankings, along with other rankings that are available through subscription databases. They identify discrepancies in rankings among these different resources, and brainstorm the reasons for these differences.
- For a more advanced activity, students investigate the various metrics that journal ranking systems employ and discuss the value of each of the metrics.

DISCUSSION QUESTIONS

- Why do journal rankings matter?
- What is the role of journal rankings in scholarly research?
- What criteria are used to rank journals? Do you think this is a fair ranking system?
- Do studies published in higher-ranked journals get more attention than those published in lower-ranked journals?
- Are higher-ranked journals considered more authoritative?
- How might journal rankings affect a tenure decision?
- Do some disciplines consider journal rankings more important than other disciplines do? Why might this be the case?
- Could journal rankings harm the scholarly research process? If so, how?
- Would certain groups of people have a more difficult time publishing in higher-ranked journals? If so, why?
- Could journal rankings cause ethical dilemmas for scholars?
- Where can you find journal rankings? Do some rankings seem more reliable than others? If so, why is that?
- What are the consequences of there being more than one journal-ranking system?
- What is the history of journal rankings? Why were they started?

PREDATORY JOURNALS

A "predatory" journal is a scholarly journal that charges authors publishing fees without providing the peer review and editing services that legitimate journals provide. They are usually poor-quality journals that trick authors into publishing with them to make money off them. The topic of these journals may be most appropriate for students who plan to attend graduate school or take part in scholarly research in some other way. However, it also illustrates a darker side to the scholarly research ecosystem, one that is likely unknown to undergraduates. A discussion or lesson on predatory journals would give you an occasion to inject a dose of reality into what might otherwise appear to those on the outside to be a faultless system. Keep in mind that whether a journal should be categorized as "predatory" or not can be a grey area. Students will need to be comfortable with some degree of ambiguity when tackling this topic.

ACTIVITY IDEAS

- After exploring several journals that could be described as "predatory," students brainstorm the factors that can make a journal seem predatory. They then apply those factors to well-respected journals in order to determine if they may have misjudged something or if their instincts were correct.
- Collect e-mail solicitations that you and your colleagues have received from what you would consider predatory journals, and have students examine the e-mails for clues that the journals in question might not be legitimate.

DISCUSSION QUESTIONS

- What does the term *predatory* indicate to you?
- Can you think of comparisons to other things that "prey" on you?
- How do predatory journals fit into the scholarly research ecosystem?
- Can you determine who or what publishes predatory journals?
- How might cultural differences influence the acceptability of predatory journals?
- Would certain groups of people be more vulnerable to solicitations from predatory journals than others? If so, why is that?
- How can you identify these types of journals? Are there specific characteristics that can identify a predatory journal?
- Are the articles published in predatory journals subject to the peer-review process? How could you find this out for specific journals?
- What sorts of damage could predatory journals cause to scholarly research?
- Many predatory journals require a payment from the author in order to publish. How might this cause an ethical dilemma?

INSTITUTIONAL REPOSITORIES

An institutional repository (IR) is an archive that collects, stores, and disseminates digital copies of the research materials created at a college, university, or other research institution. The materials are usually made available on an open-access basis. In a discussion on open-access publishing practices, institutional repositories offer a convincing case for scholars to retain at least some of the copyrights to their published research—specifically, the right to donate a copy of their research to an institutional repository, under certain conditions. Under the appropriate copyright agreements with publishers, institutional repositories allow scholars to share their research with a wider audience than the research that lives behind paywalls. They are also places where researchers can take part in scholarly conversations outside of published papers, through conference presentations and proceedings, white papers, data, and more. Of particular interest to students, depending on the policies of the individual repository, is the fact that undergraduate research can be submitted to these repositories.

ACTIVITY IDEAS

- The simple act of having students explore an institutional repository would be worthwhile. You could focus the exercise by asking them to find research in particular disciplines, formats (e.g., peer-reviewed article, conference proceedings), or from specific individuals that you know have shared their research in an IR.
- Because Google Scholar indexes the materials deposited in institutional repositories, you can have the students search for items in Google Scholar that have been deposited in an IR. This helps to emphasize how IRs can promote scholarly research, sharing it with the largest audience possible.

DISCUSSION QUESTIONS

- What is an institutional repository?
- Does every college and university have an IR?
- Why do colleges and universities maintain IRs?
- Is an IR considered open access?
- Can any faculty member or student deposit material in your university's IR?
- What sorts of materials can be found in an IR?
- How is an IR different than a library database or Google Scholar? How is it similar?
- What are the benefits to scholars from using an IR?
- Do subscription-based journals have rules about what can be shared in an IR? If so, where can you find this information?

- How are IRs important to scholarly research?
- Have any of your professors deposited their research in the university's IR? How can you determine this?
- Do you have something that could be deposited in the university's IR? Do you know how to go about doing this?
- What person or group on campus is responsible for maintaining the IR?

GOOGLE SCHOLAR

Google Scholar is a freely accessible search engine that provides a way to conduct broad searches across disciplines for scholarly literature and academic resources. Although they were wary of it in its early days, over the years libraries and librarians have accepted the usefulness of Google Scholar. A large number of faculty members and graduate students now embrace it as their go-to "database." For undergraduates, you probably see a mixed bag—some use it, while others have yet to hear about it. For those undergraduates who use it, the chances are slim that they fully understand what they are searching. If given an opportunity to talk with undergraduates about Google Scholar, you should aim to cut off any misperceptions at the pass.

ACTIVITY IDEAS

- For students who have some knowledge of both Google Scholar and subscription databases, have them brainstorm the pros and cons of using each. To make it a more focused activity, create a variety of scenarios in order for students to choose *when* one might be better to use than the other.
- Provide students with citations to search for in Google Scholar. Choose resources that offer open-access links, as well as others that display a full-text link indicating its availability from the university library. Include one or two particularly challenging examples. At the least, this type of exercise allows students an opportunity to practice navigating Google Scholar results in multiple scenarios.

DISCUSSION QUESTIONS

- What is the purpose of Google Scholar?
- What types of information does Google Scholar provide?
- In what ways do the results on Google Scholar differ from results from Google?
- How does Google Scholar define the word *scholarly*?
- Google Scholar is an index to scholarly resources. What is an index?
- How often is Google Scholar updated?
- How does Google Scholar gather its citations and its links to resources?

- Does Google Scholar share a list of all the journals that it indexes?
- Do you have access to all the resources that Google Scholar cites?
- Are all resources available via Google Scholar intended to be free?
- What special access do you, as a college student, have to the sources that are available on Google Scholar?
- Is the information available through Google Scholar reliable and credible?
- Are all of the articles found via Google Scholar peer-reviewed?
- How is Google Scholar different than a library database? How is it similar?
- Is Google Scholar sufficient for your scholarly research?
- How is Google Scholar important to scholarly research?

DISSEMINATION AND ACCESS INEQUITIES

We know that due to severe and systemic social and economic inequities in our society, certain groups of people have fewer opportunities to enter and succeed in academia, therefore limiting the voices heard within the scholarly research ecosystem. Although this topic is only part of a broader issue in our society, a discussion about its effects on the scholarly research ecosystem could be enlightening for undergraduates. The activities related to this topic should be approached with a keen awareness of the demographics of a particular class and should be conducted in a sensitive manner.

ACTIVITY IDEAS

- Ask students to consider the reasons why it can be difficult for groups of people such as women, people of color, and those within the LGBTQ community to enter academia and take part in scholarly research. Continue with a brainstorming session on the effects this problem can have on the scholarly conversation.
- Have the students role-play as faculty members who are looking for two or three peer-reviewed articles, all of which end with a paywall. Although these articles could likely be obtained from other libraries through interlibrary loan, there are exceptions. Have the students consider the ways that paywalls that scholars fail to penetrate or that cause delays in their research progress can affect the scholarly conversation.

DISCUSSION QUESTIONS

- Do all scholars have the same opportunities to share their research? If not, what are some factors that could privilege some scholarly research over others?
- Does everyone have access to scholarly research? Why or why not? Why does this matter?

- Apart from scholarly research, what other types of information may not be equitably available to everyone?
- What factors or circumstances could prevent someone from widely sharing their own scholarly research?
- Is access to the internet required to read peer-reviewed articles? If so, how does this affect the sharing of scholarly research?
- Are there some populations or groups of people who have access to more scholarly literature than others? Why is this?
- Name some consequences of the inequities in the sharing and access to scholarly information.
- Describe strategies to expand on the voices heard in the world of scholarly research.

COPYRIGHT AND AUTHORS' RIGHTS

Copyright is a broad topic that can be tailored to a specific group of students and their learning needs, since it manifests itself in many corners of the scholarly research ecosystem. Some of those corners include dissemination practices, the scholarly conversation, the scholarly publishing industry, open access, intellectual property, plagiarism, the ethical use of information, the value of information—in other words, just about everywhere. Without going too deep into the legal complexities, a basic understanding of the purpose of copyright law—what it is, what it is not—would serve undergraduates well.

ACTIVITY IDEAS

- Though it is not covered elsewhere in this book, you should consider an activity centered on Creative Commons. The students can locate open-access articles that have various Creative Common licenses. Students can explore the Creative Commons website to find the meanings of the various licenses and gain a broad understanding of how the licenses work in concert with copyright laws.
- Assign the students several scholarly journals with differing copyright policies and ask them to locate information about copyright on the websites of the respective journals. The students can then report back and should recognize the variability of copyright policies among scholarly journals.

DISCUSSION QUESTIONS

- How would you define copyright?
- When people talk about copyright, what comes to mind?
- Do you hold the copyright to anything?
- What types of things can you copyright?

- Is copyright a law?
- Are there penalties for violating copyright?
- Where can you find information about copyright?
- As a student, have you encountered any issues related to copyright?
- Do you consider plagiarism and violating copyright to be the same thing? Explain.
- How does copyright affect scholarly research?
- Are the articles published in scholarly journals copyrighted? If so, who owns the copyright?
- Do authors give up their copyright when they publish in peer-reviewed journals?
- Do scholarly publishers treat authors fairly when it comes to copyright?
- Name some reasons why an author would want to retain their copyright to a peer-reviewed article.
- Would any particular groups of people be more likely to give up their copyrights than others? If so, for what reasons?
- Is there a place on campus that can help with copyright issues?

NOTES

1. Association of College & Research Libraries, *Framework for Information Literacy for Higher Education*, www.ala.org/acrl/standards/ilframework.
2. Sherpa Romeo, "Sherpa Romeo Search," Jisc, https://v2.sherpa.ac.uk/romeo/search.html.

CHAPTER 7

ON CAMPUS

The lessons in this chapter familiarize undergraduates with the units, services, and people on college and university campuses that sustain the scholarly research ecosystem. The chapter also offers explanations to students about the research component attached to many faculty positions. How you choose to apply these lessons will depend on the campus culture at your institution.

LESSON 28

THE RESEARCH UNIVERSITY

SUMMARY

In this lesson, students learn about the campus units that support the research mission of a research university, and consider scenarios in which certain people may need additional information about the research infrastructure of the university.

SKILL LEVEL

Novice

CONTEXT

The research university performs a significant function in the scholarly research ecosystem. From the research university come peer-reviewed articles, patents, future faculty members and scholars, and graduates who find work in the private research sector. These outcomes and achievements happen because of the massive infrastructure created and maintained by research universities. This lesson introduces undergraduates to this infrastructure—academic departments, research offices, libraries, grant writers, graduate research assistants—and provides an overview of the countless offices and personnel who work in tandem to make the research university function effectively. If this seems overwhelming for your students, several other lessons in this book focus on the elements of the infrastructure individually. But no matter how you choose to approach it, this topic could be broached early in the career of an undergraduate.

LEARNING OUTCOME

The students learn about the people, offices, and services on campus that support the research mission of the university in order to get a sense of the breadth and scope of infrastructure that is needed to conduct scholarly research.

PREPARATION

Write questions that can be answered from information found online about the scholarly research ecosystem on your campus, or another campus if needed. Prepare a slip of paper with a different question for each pair of students. Possible questions that can be tailored to align with your local situation include:

- What is the research mission of your university? Find specific examples of ways the university is fulfilling this mission.
- What are some examples of offices or departments on campus that exist to support the university's research mission?
- The Office of Research is dedicated to promoting and managing research on campus. What can you learn from its website about the responsibilities of the staff who work in this office?
- The Office of Grants coordinates all research grants on campus. Find at least three specific examples of the responsibilities of this office.
- What is the key purpose of the Office of Human Subject Research? Name at least three examples of how this office supports the university's research mission.
- What sorts of research-related positions can you find advertised on the university's employment website?
- There are many research labs on campus. Find information about the Psychology labs. Can you determine how the labs are funded? Do they hire graduate students? What about undergraduates?
- In what ways do the university library and its librarians support the research mission of the university?
- The university has an outreach office in every county in the state. Name at least two ways that these offices help to fulfill the research mission of the university.

Include on the slip of paper a link to an online form (such as a Google Form) where students can enter their answers to these questions. In preparation for the second activity, you will create scenarios that will give students an opportunity to dig deeper into specific aspects of the research university. Create a slide deck with one scenario per slide. Example scenarios include:

- You're a student interested in attending graduate school in Chemistry at this university. What are three importance pieces of information you should know about the university before you apply?
- You're a historian with an upcoming job interview at this university. You specialize in eighteenth-century religious history. What services should you ask about during your interview to ensure the university can support your research?
- You're a grant writer for the department of economics. What are two other offices, services, or people on campus that support your work as a grant writer?

The students will require internet access to complete the activities in this lesson. Here are some additional ideas as you prepare:

- Following a discussion of their findings in Activity One, have the students sketch an organizational scheme for the university, drawing lines between crucial collaborations, prioritizing the importance of the different elements, or categorizing similar things, such as people, offices, and services.
- You should only use three or four broad questions for Activity One, and then give the students a chance to converse about their unique responses.

- Have the students compare the research infrastructure of their university to another research university, citing the similarities and differences.
- Rather than students searching the web for information, have them conduct online interviews with staff in the various offices on campus in order to answer the questions.

INSTRUCTION

ACTIVITY ONE: EXPLORING THE RESEARCH UNIVERSITY

Group work, class discussion, 15 to 20 minutes

Explain to students the plan for the day and after dividing the class into pairs, distribute a pre-prepared question to each pair. Give the students sufficient time to explore the university website to locate answers to the questions. If the online form feeds into a spreadsheet, display the spreadsheet after the activity has been completed so that students can see and comment on the questions and responses of their classmates.

ACTIVITY TWO: QUESTIONS ABOUT THE UNIVERSITY

Group work, class discussion, 15 to 20 minutes

Pull up the slide deck and organize the students into groups of three or four. Provide paper or have students enter their responses to each of the scenarios in an online form. Ask each group to share their responses to one of the scenarios.

ASSESSMENT PROMPT

"Of the many offices, people, and services that we discussed today, name a specific one that you believe to be particularly critical to the research mission of the university. Justify your response."

LESSON 29

SHOW ME THE GRANT MONEY

SUMMARY

Students brainstorm the reasons why scholars apply for research grants, learn about entities that bestow grants, and role-play as scholars who must find appropriate grants for a research project.

SKILL LEVEL

Intermediate to Advanced

CONTEXT

Competition for grant money among research universities is fierce. For researchers, achieving tenure often hinges on securing external grant money; for universities, research grants boost their reputation and prestige, helping them to recruit high-quality and diverse students and faculty. Despite the importance that research universities place on grant money, and the resources that universities invest in personnel and offices dedicated to writing and managing grants, undergraduates may be unaware of the behind-the-scenes scramble to finance research on campus. Gaining an awareness of this can provide undergraduates with a clearer understanding of the scholarly research ecosystem on campus, and especially an appreciation of the possible expectations of them if they choose to attend graduate school and later enter academia as a profession. Grant money can originate from private corporations and organizations, as gifts, from endowments, and as part of federal and state funding. In an effort to try and keep things simple, though, this lesson zeros in on one major grantor, the United States government.

LEARNING OUTCOME

The students will learn about the role that grants play in the funding of scholarly research in order to recognize their presence in the scholarly research process.

PREPARATION

For Activity One, have the research mission of your university or another one on hand, and prepare a slide with the instructions "Find an example of a current research project happening on campus in your assigned disciplinary area. Can you determine how the research is being funded?" How you prepare for this first activity will depend on the volume of grant-funded research that is taking place at your university and the ease with which someone can find information about these research projects and funding online. If this proves to be difficult, rather than challenging the students to find examples of university research on their own, provide them with the examples, and then have the students focus on locating information about the granting agencies instead.

In preparation for the second activity, develop at least three research topics that would align with potential governmental grants. Ideally, you should write at least one research question based in each of the broad liberal arts categories: humanities, social sciences, and sciences. Each group of three or four students will need access to the "Research Grants" worksheet (worksheet 7.1).

Here are some additional ideas as you prepare:

- In Activity One, rather than a broad focus on the liberal arts, have the students explore specific fields of research. They could also survey research in specific professional fields.
- In Activity One, allow the students to share the titles of some of the more creative or interesting grants that they locate.
- Spend time discussing why the U.S. government offers grant money.

INSTRUCTION

ACTIVITY ONE: GRANT SUPPORT ON CAMPUS

Class discussion, 15 to 20 minutes

Review the research mission of the university with students and then begin with a basic set of questions to get students talking.

- Who or what finances the research that happens on campus?

The responses to this question may vary, but if students fail to list research grants, introduce grants as a main source of research funding. If needed, provide a definition of *grant* in the context of scholarly research.

- Why do researchers apply for grant money? To hire assistants? To purchase lab equipment? To travel to research locations or conferences?

Entertain all pertinent responses that the students provide.

Display the pre-prepared slide and explain to the class that they will investigate grant-funded research on campus. Divide the class into thirds. Instruct one-third of the class to search the university website for examples of research projects happening in the sciences, another third to do the same for social sciences, and the last third to focus on the humanities. Depending on what the students already know about the liberal arts, they may need more direction, so be prepared to provide examples of disciplines within each of the categories. Also, it would be helpful to model a search for the students on how to find information about university research, with an emphasis on locating information about the funding of the research. After giving an appropriate amount of time for students to explore online, ask them to respond to the question on the pre-prepared slide (see "Preparation" above). Depending on the examples that they locate, you may need to fill in gaps as to the entities that fund research. Discussion questions include:

- How does what you and your classmates found regarding grant funding on campus change or confirm your perception of how the university supports its research mission?
- Can you think of alternative ways that the university could fund research in the absence of research grants?

Explain that for the sake of keeping things simple and also because of the prestige attached to obtaining one, the next activity will focus on research grants funded by the U.S. government.

ACTIVITY TWO: FINDING GOVERNMENT GRANTS

Group work, 20 to 25 minutes

Introduce students to the website Grants.gov, and explain its role as the main portal for locating U.S. government grants.[1] Perform a few searches for the class and show them the various ways they can refine their search results. For example, the website allows users to limit by Category, such as "Education" or "Natural Resources," as well as by agency, such as NASA, the National Endowment for the Arts, and the Department of Justice. Give students a few minutes to explore the site. Keep in mind that for the purposes of this exercise, students should learn about the existence of this website and the large number of grants available, not details about grant applications and such.

Next, organize the students into groups of three or four and ask the groups to number off to three. Give each group a "Research Grants" worksheet (worksheet 7.1) and display the slide with the pre-prepared research questions. Give the groups an opportunity to share what they found. Likely the groups searching for science grants will list the same three grants, as will be the same for the groups working with topics in the social sciences and humanities.

ASSESSMENT PROMPT

"Do you consider securing a grant part of the research process? Explain why or why not."

WORKSHEET 7.1

RESEARCH GRANTS

You and your partners have formed a research group for the purpose of conducting research on your assigned topic.

As we just practiced, search the Grants.gov site for grants that could help fund your assigned research project.

List a couple of ways that you limited or refined your results.

Judging by the title of the grants only, choose three that your research group should further investigate.

LESSON 30

PROTECTING HUMANS

SUMMARY

Through class discussion, students learn basic information about human subjects research protections. They role-play in order to get a sense of the different categories of review conducted by Institutional Review Boards.

SKILL LEVEL

Intermediate to Advanced

CONTEXT

The term *human subjects research* denotes any scientific investigation that involves living human beings as research subjects. Most research universities have an Institutional Review Board (IRB), comprised of faculty members on campus, that oversees the various ethical issues and regulatory requirements involving human subjects research. Research universities also maintain an office or unit tasked with coordinating and managing this work, ensuring that the university follows the appropriate rules and regulations that apply to human subjects research. These regulations and policies cover a wide area, from biomedical research with its use of human tissue to educational research and the assessment of achievement tests. This "IRB process" represents an important piece of the scholarly research ecosystem. Undergraduates may have heard of the infamous Tuskegee Syphilis study or Henrietta Lacks's immortal cells.[2] They may not realize, however, that these inexcusable ethical violations would not (or should not) happen today due to the federal regulations that protect human research subjects. Extreme examples like the Tuskegee study can provide a lead-in for discussions with students on this complex topic, with its unfamiliar terms such as *informed consent*, *special and vulnerable populations*, *exemptions*, and *full board review*. In this lesson, students will learn about the protections afforded human research subjects by federal and university policies, and will also get a sense of the types of research that require IRB approval.

LEARNING OUTCOME

Students will learn about the review process for human subjects research in order to recognize its function in protecting humans who are the subject of research studies.

PREPARATION

If possible, locate a brief video that describes an example of research that harmed human subjects. An example of this research would most likely have happened prior to the *Belmont Report* (1978).[3] Also, prepare a slide deck that will give students a brief overview of the purpose of the review process for human subjects research. Possible topics for the slides include:

- The purpose of human subjects research regulations
- The role of the federal government in such regulations
- The Office of Human Subjects Research on campus
- The purpose of Institutional Review Boards
- The different categories of review (exempt, expedited, and full-board review)

Develop a variety of research scenarios, such as those presented in the "Human Subjects" worksheet (worksheet 7.2), which will challenge the students to determine if a research project would be deemed exempt from review, qualify for an expedited review, or require a full-board review. A closer examination of the three different categories in this way should reinforce to students the reasons why humans need protection in the course of scientific research involving them. This lesson requires internet access.

Here are some additional ideas to consider as you prepare:

- Some of the Collaborative Institutional Training Initiative (CITI) training modules would provide context for students and could be completed before the session using the flipped-classroom method.
- If your campus lacks an office for human subjects research, direct students to the federal Office for Human Research Protections, from which universities pull much of the information on their websites.[4]

INSTRUCTION

ACTIVITY ONE: HUMAN SUBJECTS RESEARCH

Class discussion, 15 to 20 minutes

Using the pre-prepared slide deck, gauge what the students know about human subjects research. Emphasize to the students that all research universities must follow the prescribed regulations and the IRB process.

ACTIVITY TWO: CATEGORIES OF REVIEW

Group work, class discussion, 15 to 20 minutes

Either direct students to the university web page that contains information about human subjects research guidelines, including a description of the three categories of IRB review, or provide them with print copies that describe the three categories. Give each pair of students a "Human Subjects" worksheet (worksheet 7.2). After students complete the worksheet, give them the opportunity to share their responses with one another.

ASSESSMENT PROMPT

"Describe one way in which human research subjects could be harmed in the absence of federal regulations and Institutional Review Boards."

WORKSHEET 7.2

HUMAN SUBJECTS

Work with your partner to complete this worksheet. Be prepared to share your responses with your classmates.

Scenario 1: You're both graduate students studying early childhood education who want to research whether positive reinforcement in the classroom has a direct relationship to passing grades. Your target population are first-graders.

Which category of IRB review will this research require? Why?

Scenario 2: The pharmaceutical research group that you're both members of would like to test an experimental drug on pregnant women to measure its efficacy in reducing morning sickness.

Which category of IRB review will this research require? Why?

Scenario 3: As market researchers, you want to ask customers at a local grocery store to take an anonymous survey on their shopping habits.

Which category of IRB review will this research require? Why?

LESSON 31

THE VALUE OF THE LIBRARY

SUMMARY

Students share ways that they use the university library and then brainstorm how the library supports the research mission of the university.

SKILL LEVEL

Novice to Intermediate

CONTEXT

The value of the university library derives from two critical things: its information resources, and the people who work at the library. First, let us consider how faculty members value the library. Because of the instantaneous methods of information-gathering we have become accustomed to, and the sleek seamlessness of this process made possible by search engines, library collections, link resolvers, and authentication methods, it should come as no surprise that faculty often assume that the materials they find online are "free." In fact, faculty members have been known to say that they rarely use the library to find materials, although they search Google Scholar and then link to full-text articles that the library subscribes to on a daily basis. The complex arrangements that libraries make with journal publishers may be on the radars of some faculty members, but not all. Some faculty members see the library as a purely physical space, with excellent interlibrary loan services and friendly librarians, without being aware that the library's resources are available to them because the library purchases subscriptions to those resources. In addition to the information resources available, the faculty view librarians as helpful and responsive to requests for information resources. However, librarians must continuously market their other services, such as information literacy instruction, as well as evolving services like scholarly communication and data management. Now that we have considered how faculty value the library, think about what undergraduates know about the library's value—probably much less, thereby justifying the inclusion of this lesson. Of course, the audience for this book can always teach sessions on the value of the library on the fly, but it is helpful to highlight the vital role the library plays in facilitating research. The university library is an essential part of the infrastructure of the scholarly research ecosystem.

LEARNING OUTCOME

Students will learn the ways that the library supports scholarly research on campus in order to recognize how the library and librarians can support them when they work on their own research projects.

PREPARATION

For the first activity, prepare a discussion question using an audience response tool, such as "Describe one way that you use the library." You should also prepare a slide with the following instructions: "Explore the library website and find two additional services or resources that you didn't know about that would help you with your research assignments." In preparation for Activity Two, create a list of all the services that the library provides which could benefit faculty members who conduct research. Each group of three or four students will need access to the "List of Library Services" worksheet (worksheet 7.3), tailored to align with the services provided by your library. Because the students will be ranking items, it may be more efficient to use an online form that allows for this option than a print worksheet. This lesson requires internet access.

INSTRUCTION

ACTIVITY ONE: STUDENT USE OF THE LIBRARY

Class discussion, individual work, 15 to 20 minutes

Using the audience response tool, the students share anonymously one way in which they use the library. Take time to review all of the responses. Call attention to the similarities and differences in their responses. Then pull up the pre-prepared slide and give the students time to individually explore the library website. If available, direct the students to a services page or an online guide, to help them in answering the slide's question. Their answers will likely range widely. For this activity, anything new that students can walk away with should be helpful. Be sure to share with the class how librarians can assist with research, as well as the services and programs that are targeted to undergraduates.

ACTIVITY TWO: SUPPORTING THE RESEARCH MISSION

Class discussion, 20 to 25 minutes

Explain to the students: "Now that we have discussed some ways that you use the library, let's now think about the ways that the library supports research and the research mission of the university. Of the things that you listed as helping you do your research in the first activity, which of those do you believe could be applied to the faculty on campus who conduct research? Which of those services would benefit them?"

Organize the students into groups of two or three and provide each group with a copy of the "List of Library Services" worksheet (worksheet 7.3). Review the purpose of the activity with the students. Once they have completed the activity, if they entered their responses into an online form, display the results for students to see and discuss. Ask a couple of follow-up questions:

- Do you think any of these services are not necessary?
- Are there any services listed here that are new to you?

ASSESSMENT PROMPT

"What do you believe to be the most important service provided by the library in support of the research mission of the university?"

WORKSHEET 7.3

LIST OF LIBRARY SERVICES

Compromise with your teammates to rank the library services listed below based on the importance of each in supporting faculty research (most important to least important). For those services unfamiliar to you, search for information about them online to help you determine where to rank them in importance.

_____ Searching library databases for peer-reviewed articles

_____ Searching the library catalog for books

_____ Making interlibrary loan requests

_____ Setting up privileges so that faculty graduate assistants can check out information resources from the library in the faculty member's name

_____ Purchasing books and other information resources

_____ Developing a data management plan

_____ Consulting on the best journals in which to publish research

_____ Identifying open access journals and the copyright policies of these journals

_____ Researching scholarly journal rankings

_____ Investigating whether a solicitation email is from a predatory journal

_____ Completing the "library resources" section of grant applications

_____ Assisting in setting up an online scholarly profile

_____ Offering workshops on how to use citation management software

_____ Helping to gather scholarly research for a literature review

_____ Researching potential grant funding for a research project

_____ Teaching research skills to faculty graduate assistants

LESSON 32

UNDERGRADUATE RESEARCH

SUMMARY

In this lesson the students think about their research interests, explore research opportunities for undergraduates, and brainstorm appropriate strategies for asking a professor to serve as their research mentor.

SKILL LEVEL

Novice to Intermediate

CONTEXT

Many research universities have programs that promote and support research by undergraduates. The literature validates the effectiveness of these programs, and a number of authoritative institutions, such as the National Science Foundation in its Research Experiences for Undergraduates program, also serve to legitimize this effort. Undergraduates who enter college from preparatory schools or have followed advanced placement and college prep tracks in high school may know about these sorts of programs. Most other undergraduates will not, however. Accordingly, this lesson introduces students to the concept of undergraduate research. In the absence of a formal program on campus, having at least an awareness of the concept could empower students to approach faculty members about their research interests; just be sure that the faculty culture at your institution would support this sort of proactive approach by students.

LEARNING OUTCOME

The students will learn about undergraduate research on campus in order to gain awareness of the opportunities for them in this area.

PREPARATION

Using an audience response tool, prepare a question about the research interests of the students, such as "What is something that, if not restricted by time or money, you would like to research now?" Give students the option to include their name with their response if they choose. For the second activity, each student will need a copy of the "Undergraduate

Research" worksheet (worksheet 7.4). Because this activity depends heavily on your local situation, edit the worksheet as needed. The worksheet asks students to create an individualized plan for pursuing a research project under the guidance of a faculty member, so you should let the students take the worksheet with them when they leave class. If you plan to use the worksheet as an assessment tool, consider using carbonless paper; this will allow students to take a copy and you can keep a copy as well.

Here are some additional ideas as you prepare:

- Survey the research interests of the students before the session and then scout out faculty members online whose research aligns with those interests. This information can be added to the worksheets in order to give students a more defined starting point for the second activity.
- Often undergraduate research office websites will spotlight successful research projects. Share examples of these with your students to serve as inspiration and spark research ideas.
- If you have access to the students after the session, give them feedback on the plans they created in the second activity.
- For those students who are serious about undergraduate research opportunities, encourage them to reach out to the faculty member they identified, or to the undergraduate research office and, if they are willing and comfortable, ask them to report back to their classmates about the experience.

INSTRUCTION

ACTIVITY ONE: UNDERGRADUATE RESEARCH AS A CONCEPT

Class discussion, 15 to 20 minutes

Begin by surveying the students about their research interests, using the audience-response tool. Take time to engage with them on their topics. Next, ask them to consider how they might pursue this sort of research if not given the chance to do so in a particular course. Continue by asking the class, "If given the opportunity, how might pursuing this research interest outside of a formal course benefit you?" The students will likely mention gaining research experience, strengthening their resumes, and increasing their chances of acceptance to graduate school as potential benefits. Guide the conversation to ways that the faculty can also benefit from this sort of arrangement. For instance, "How are some ways the faculty might benefit by partnering with undergraduates like yourself on research projects?" The answers to this question may not come as easily, so help the students brainstorm. Advancing faculty members' research and enabling them to gain additional experience in teaching and mentorship—both activities that would be judged positively during tenure reviews—are suggestions. Lastly, have the class think about the ways that undergraduate research benefits the university. The answers might include contributing to the mission of the university, boosting the reputation of the university, and attracting high-quality students and faculty.

ACTIVITY TWO: GETTING INVOLVED

Individual work, group work, class discussion, 20 to 25 minutes

Organize the class into partners of two and provide each student with an "Undergraduate Research" worksheet (worksheet 7.4). After a sufficient amount of time, ask the partners to swap and provide feedback to each other for the last question on the worksheet. With the remaining time, solicit volunteers to share their plans with the class.

ASSESSMENT

If you use carbonless paper or an electronic form, review the students' responses on the worksheet to see if they made correct choices and developed an appropriate plan.

WORKSHEET 7.4

UNDERGRADUATE RESEARCH

For question 1, work with your partner to find the answers. Each of you should record the answers on your own worksheet, though. For questions 2 through 4, work individually. After the allotted time is up, you'll be asked to swap and provide your partner feedback on question 4.

1. Locate the Office of Undergraduate Research on campus. What are some ways you could contribute to scholarly research on campus through this office? If you wanted to learn more, is there a contact person at the office? What sort of information or instructions do they provide on what to do?

2. Is there a faculty member on campus that is doing research similar to your interests? If not, is there a faculty member in the department that serves as a contact for undergraduate students?

3. What are some strategies for contacting the faculty member you identified in the question above? Do they provide a link for contacting them? Do they encourage e-mail?

4. Considering what you can learn about the faculty member online, develop a three-step plan on the most appropriate way to contact them about your research interests. Think about what the faculty member needs to know about you, your research interest, and what you hope to gain from having them as a mentor.

Feedback from your partner:

LESSON 33

PUBLISH OR PERISH

SUMMARY

The students brainstorm facts and features regarding the academic tenure system. They consider the effects this system may have on scholarly research by analyzing examples of the research requirements for tenure from various departments across their campus.

SKILL LEVEL

Advanced

CONTEXT

Undergraduates most likely learn at some point in their college careers about the peer-review process and how it results in the gold standard for research. However, they may not have considered certain motivational factors driving faculty members' decisions about what to research and where to publish, and in particular, the motivation of faculty members to secure their livelihood by achieving tenure. Some voices both inside and outside of academia have expressed mixed feelings about the academic tenure system and the familiar adage "publish or perish." This critical scrutiny of the system can be found in journals, websites, and blogs focused on higher education. Regardless of these opinions, tenure continues to hold a sacred place within academia and the scholarly research ecosystem. Due to the number of issues surrounding tenure, you could tackle it several ways in the classroom. From an ethical standpoint, you might address the exploitative nature of contingent non-tenure-track appointments, or the discriminatory nature of some tenure decisions. Or you can take it in a different direction, with an examination of the influence that tenure has on scholarly conversations and communication. For example, a faculty member might choose to delay a longitudinal study with potential groundbreaking findings because the project could not be completed before their tenure deadline. In another instance, a grant that aligns with the research program of a scholar may fall short of the dollar amount needed to achieve tenure, so they redirect their focus to obtaining a larger grant on another research topic. This lesson offers foundational knowledge about academic tenure that can be built upon by considering some of these complex issues.

LEARNING OUTCOME

The students will learn about the research components of achieving tenure in order to appreciate the role of the tenure system within the scholarly research ecosystem.

PREPARATION

Be prepared with answers for the discussion prompts in Activity One. For the second activity, obtain tenure requirements that include scholarly research for the faculty on your campus or another campus. An internet search will provide a deluge of possible examples of these requirements. Try to obtain examples from the humanities, social sciences, sciences, and professional programs, if possible; or you could narrow the focus to one specific discipline, depending on the interest of the students in the class. To give them a true sense of the tenure system, choose some requirements that are specific—for example, a faculty member must publish five peer-reviewed journals in top-tier journals—as well as some requirements that are more general. Choose enough requirements so that each group of three to four students has a different set of them; because each student will need a copy of the requirements, however, you may want to provide URLs to the documents rather than paper copies. For extensive documents, be prepared to direct the students to the section they should focus on. Each group will need a copy of the "Tenure Requirements" worksheet (worksheet 7.5). You may want to adjust the questions on the worksheet to better align with the documentation, if this is helpful.

INSTRUCTION

ACTIVITY ONE: UNDERSTANDING TENURE

Class discussion, 10 to 15 minutes

Begin by presenting a few warm-up questions:

- Have the heard of the term *tenure*, as in someone receiving or obtaining tenure?
- Did you hear the term used in high school? What about your time in college so far?
- Why would a faculty member want to achieve tenure?
- How would you define tenure in this context?
- What are some benefits of tenure?
- What must faculty members do in order to achieve tenure?
- What happens if a faculty member fails to obtain tenure?

As a result of this discussion, the students should have a sense of the meaning and purpose of academic tenure.

ACTIVITY TWO: TENURE AND SCHOLARLY RESEARCH

Group work, class discussion, 20 to 25 minutes

Break the class up into groups of three or four and hand each group the "Tenure Requirements" worksheet (worksheet 7.5). Provide the students with their assigned tenure requirements, whether in print or electronic form, and then review the instructions on the worksheet. After the students complete the activity and following a class discussion of their responses, broach a few open-ended questions about the overall tenure system:

- How does this system benefit the university?
- Do you see any potential problems with this system in relation to scholarly research?
- How might this system influence what is published in scholarly journals?

ASSESSMENT PROMPT

"Provide an example of how the academic tenure system can affect how faculty members prioritize their research."

NOTES

1. Grants.gov, Program Management Office, "Search Grants," www.grants.gov/web/grants/search-grants.html.
2. Tuskegee University, Tuskegee University Bioethics Center, "About the USPHS Syphilis Study," www.tuskegee.edu/about-us/centers-of-excellence/bioethics-center/about-the-usphs-syphilis-study; Johns Hopkins Medicine, "Honoring Henrietta: The Legacy of Henrietta Lacks," www.hopkinsmedicine.org/henriettalacks.
3. U.S. Department of Health, Education, and Welfare, National Commission for the Protection of Human Subjects of Biomedical and Behavioral Research, *The Belmont Report*, published April 18, 1979, www.hhs.gov/ohrp/regulations-and-policy/belmont-report/index.html.
4. U.S. Department of Health, Education, and Welfare, Office for Human Research Protections, "About OHRP," last modified February 12, 2016, https://www.hhs.gov/ohrp/about-ohrp.

WORKSHEET 7.5

TENURE REQUIREMENTS

Take a few minutes and read over the tenure requirements or guidelines for your assigned department. Pay special attention to the scholarly research requirements. After two or three minutes, come together and answer the questions on this worksheet as a group.

In order to get tenure in the _____ department, what must faculty contribute in the form of scholarly research?

Publish peer-reviewed articles? If so, how many?

Give presentations or talks at academic conferences?

Publish in specific journals? If so, what kinds?

Publish in scholarly journals with low acceptance rank? If so, why would this matter?

In addition to scholarly research, list some other job responsibilities or tasks someone in this department must do to achieve tenure.

Prepare to give a brief presentation to your classmates on the tenure requirements of your assigned department. All group members should participate.

BIBLIOGRAPHY

Association of College & Research Libraries. *Framework for Information Literacy for Higher Education.* 2015. www.ala.org/acrl/standards/ilframework.

Association of College & Research Libraries, Scholarly Communications Committee. "Scholarly Communication." 2003. www.ala.org/acrl/publications/whitepapers/principlesstrategies.

Bowles-Terry, Melissa, and Cassandra Kvenild. *Classroom Assessment Techniques for Librarians.* Chicago: Association of College & Research Libraries, 2015.

Creswell, John W., and J. David Creswell. *Research Design: Qualitative, Quantitative, and Mixed Methods Approaches.* 5th ed. Los Angeles: SAGE, 2018.

Grants.gov, Program Management Office. "Search Grants." www.grants.gov/web/grants/search-grants.html.

Haig, Brian D. "Scientific Method." In *Sage Reference Encyclopedia of Research Design,* edited by Neil J. Salkind, 1326–29. Thousand Oaks, CA: SAGE, 2010.

Johns Hopkins Medicine. "Honoring Henrietta: The Legacy of Henrietta Lacks." www.hopkinsmedicine.org/henriettalacks/.

Lupton, Mandy, and Christine Susan Bruce. "Windows on Information Literacy Worlds: Generic, Situated and Transformative Perspectives." In *Practising Information Literacy: Bringing Theories of Learning, Practice and Information Literacy Together*, edited by Annemaree Lloyd and Sanna Talja, 3–27. Wagga Wagga, New South Wales: Charles Stuart University, 2010.

Sherpa Romeo. "Sherpa Romeo Search." Jisc. https://v2.sherpa.ac.uk/romeo/search.html.

Tuskegee University, Tuskegee University Bioethics Center. "About the USPHS Syphilis Study." www.tuskegee.edu/about-us/centers-of-excellence/bioethics-center/about-the-usphs-syphilis-study.

U.S. Department of Health and Human Services, Office for Human Research Protections. "About OHRP." Last modified February 12, 2016. https://www.hhs.gov/ohrp/about-ohrp.

U.S. Department of Health, Education, and Welfare. National Commission for the Protection of Human Subjects of Biomedical and Behavioral Research. *The Belmont Report.* Published April 18, 1979. www.hhs.gov/ohrp/regulations-and-policy/belmont-report/index.html.

U.S. Department of Labor, Bureau of Labor Statistics. *Occupational Outlook Handbook.* www.bls.gov/ooh.

INDEX

A
abstracts, analyzing, 2–5
access. *See* dissemination and access
applied research, 2
archival research, 82
authority
    community-granted, 36–39
    expertise versus, 36–39
    markers of, 16–19
authors' rights, 131–132

B
Barriers to Inclusivity worksheet, 46
basic research, 2
Bayesian method, 68
Belmont Report, 142

C
campus resources/concerns
    about, 133
    grant money and, 137–140
    libraries, 145–148
    protecting humans, 141–144
    publish or perish, 154–157
    research universities, 134–136
    undergraduate research, 149–153
Choosing a Scholarly Journal worksheet, 116
citations, 86–87
communication, formal versus informal, 20–21, 22–23. *See also* dissemination and access; scholarly conversations
Comparing Research in the Sciences worksheet, 99
conversation starters
    on disciplines, 108
    on dissemination and access, 126–132
    on methods of inquiry, 81–87
    on people/researchers, 47–49
    purpose of, xviii
Conversations and Communication worksheet, 112
conversations of scholars
    inclusivity and, 43–46
    on methods of inquiry, 81–87
    sharing results and, 20, 21–22
    understanding, 9–11
copyright, 128, 131–132
Creswell, John, 72, 77

D
data management, 82–84
Designing a House worksheet, 75
Designing Research worksheet, 76
digital humanities, 104–107
Digital Humanities Project worksheet, 107
disciplines
    about, 89
    conversation starters on, 108
    digital humanities, 104–107
    liberal arts, 90–95
    science research, 96–99
    social science research, 100–103
dissemination and access
    about, 109
    conversation starters on, 126–132
    inequities in, 130–131
    open access, 121–125
    scholarly journals, 110–112
    scholarly research subscriptions, 117–120
    sharing results and, 20–23
    where to publish, 113–116
diversity, 33–35
Does One Size Fit All? worksheet, 71

E
Education of Professionals worksheet, 32
exclusivity, problem of, 43–46

exemptions, 141
expertise versus authority, 36–39

F

formal communication, 20–21, 22–23
Framework for Information Literacy for Higher Education
    Authority Is Constructed and Contextual, 36
    inclusion of concepts from, xv, 1
    Information Creation as a Process, 117
    Information Has Value, 117
    iterative nature of research and, 6
    Scholarship as Conversation, 9–11, 43, 45
    Searching as Strategic Exploration, 117
full board review, 141

G

Gaining Authority worksheet, 39
Google Scholar, 12, 26, 40–42, 118, 126, 129–130, 145
graduate students, 47–48
grant money, 137–140

H

human subjects research, 141–144
Human Subjects worksheet, 144
Humanists worksheet, 93
hypothesis, 69
hypothetico-deductive method, 68

I

inclusivity, 43–46
inductive method, 68
inequities in dissemination and access, 130–131
inference, 68
informal communication, 20–21, 22–23
informed consent, 141
inquiry, as term, 62–65
institutional repositories (IR), 128–129
Institutional Review Boards (IRBs), 141–144
interdisciplinary research, 108
irreproducibility, 82

J

Journal Subscriptions worksheet, 120
journals. *See* scholarly journals
journals, scholarly
    choosing where to publish, 113–116
    job of, 110–112
    predatory journals and, 127
    rankings for, 126
    subscriptions to, 117–120

L

Lacks, Henrietta, 141
lesson outlines, xvii–xviii
lexicons, 52–54
liberal arts, 90–95
libraries, value of, 145–148
linear process, avoiding focus on, 6
List of Library Services worksheet, 148
literature reviews, 85–86
local circumstances, xvi–xvii

M

malleability of research, 6–8
methods of inquiry
    about, 67
    conversation starters on, 81–87
    quantitative versus qualitative research, 77–80
    research design, 72–76
    scientific method, 68–71
mixed methods research, 81
My Professor's Authority worksheet, 19

N

Natural Scientists worksheet, 94

O

objective-subjective distinction, 77–78
Occupational Outlook Handbook, 30
open access, 119, 121–125
Open Access Policies worksheet, 124–125
ORCID, 40

P

paywalls, 118–119
peer review, 12–15
Peer-Review Process Roles worksheet, 15
people/researchers
    about, 25
    community-granted authority, 36–39
    diversity among, 33–35
    inclusivity, 43–46
    PhDs, 29–32
    scholarly profiles, 40–42
    scholars, 26–28

PhD, path to, 29–32
predatory journals, 127
"Principles and Strategies for the Reform of Scholarly Communication," 20
profiles, scholarly, 40–42
protecting humans, 141–144
publish or perish, 154–157
publishing. *See* dissemination and access; scholarly journals
purpose of research, 2–5
Purposes of Scholarly Research worksheet, 5

Q

QUAN or QUAL worksheet, 80
quantitative versus qualitative research, 77–80

R

rankings for scholarly journals, 126
reproducibility, 82
research
 applied, 2
 archival, 82
 interdisciplinary, 108
 purpose of, 2–5
 quantitative versus qualitative, 77–80
research design, 72–76
Research Grants worksheet, 140
research methods versus research design, 72
research process
 about, 1
 iterative nature of, 6–8
 malleability of, 6–8
 markers of authority and, 16–19
 peer review and, 12–15
 purpose of, 2–5
 scholar conversations and, 9–11
 sharing results of, 20–23
Research Scenarios worksheet, 64
research universities, 134–136
results, sharing, 20–23

S

scholarly, as term, 59–61
scholarly conversations
 inclusivity and, 43–46
 sharing results and, 20, 21–22
 understanding, 9–11
scholarly journals
 choosing where to publish, 113–116
 job of, 110–112
 predatory journals and, 127
 rankings for, 126
 subscriptions to, 117–120
scholarly literature, 85–86
Scholarly Profile worksheet, 42
scholarly profiles, 40–42
scholarly research ecosystem
 on campus, 133–157
 description of, xv
 disciplines, 89–108
 dissemination and access, 109–132
 methods of inquiry, 67–87
 people, 25–49
 process, 1–23
 terminology, 51–65
scholarly research subscriptions, 117–120
scholars, defining, 26–28
science research, 96–99
scientific method, 68–71
search versus research, 62–65
Sherpa Romeo website, 121, 122
social science research, 100–103
Social Scientists worksheet, 94
source evaluation, 15, 55, 59
special populations, 141
subscriptions to scholarly journals, 117–120
support team, 48

T

teaching style, xvi
tenure
 grant money and, 137
 publish or perish, 154–157
Tenure Requirements worksheet, 157
terminology
 about, 51
 lexicons, 52–54
 scholarly, as term, 59–61
 search versus research, 62–65
 word choice, 55–58
theory, 69
Tuskegee Syphilis study, 141

U

undergraduate research, 149–153
Undergraduate Research worksheet, 152–153
United States, grant money and, 137–140

V

Value of the Social Sciences worksheet, 102–103
vocabularies/lexicons, 52–54
vulnerable populations, 141

W

Web of Science, 40
word choice, xvii, 55–58
worksheets
- Barriers to Inclusivity, 46
- Choosing a Scholarly Journal, 116
- Comparing Research in the Sciences, 99
- Conversations and Communication, 112
- Designing a House, 75
- Designing Research, 76
- Digital Humanities Project, 107
- Does One Size Fit All? 71
- Education of Professionals, 32
- Gaining Authority, 39
- Human Subjects, 144
- Humanists, 93
- Journal Subscriptions, 120
- List of Library Services, 148
- My Professor's Authority, 19
- Natural Scientists, 94
- Open Access Policies, 124–125
- Peer-Review Process Roles, 15
- Purposes of Scholarly Research, 5
- Quan or Qual, 80
- Research Grants, 140
- Research Scenarios, 64
- Scholarly Profile, 42
- Social Scientists, 94
- Tenure Requirements, 157
- Undergraduate Research, 152–153
- Value of the Social Sciences, 102–103

ALA TechSource

Learn more and subscribe at
alatechsource.org

Practical and concise, ALA TechSource publications help you

- Stay on top of emerging technologies
- Discover the latest tools proving effective in libraries
- Implement practical and time-saving strategies
- Learn from industry experts on topics such as privacy policies, online instruction, automation systems, digital preservation, artificial intelligence (AI), and more